Cambridge Elements

Elements in Money and Banking
edited by
Chao Gu
University of Missouri
Joseph Haslag
Auburn University

MIDDLEMEN IN SEARCH EQUILIBRIUM

A Survey

Grace Xun Gong
Zhejiang University

Ziqi Qiao
University of Wisconsin-Madison

Randall Wright
Zhejiang University and Wisconsin School of Business

CAMBRIDGE
UNIVERSITY PRESS

CAMBRIDGE
UNIVERSITY PRESS

Shaftesbury Road, Cambridge CB2 8EA, United Kingdom

One Liberty Plaza, 20th Floor, New York, NY 10006, USA

477 Williamstown Road, Port Melbourne, VIC 3207, Australia

314–321, 3rd Floor, Plot 3, Splendor Forum, Jasola District Centre, New Delhi – 110025, India

Cambridge University Press is part of Cambridge University Press & Assessment, a department of the University of Cambridge.

We share the University's mission to contribute to society through the pursuit of education, learning and research at the highest international levels of excellence.

www.cambridge.org
Information on this title: www.cambridge.org/9781009700306

DOI: 10.1017/9781009700313

When citing this work, please include a reference to the DOI 10.1017/9781009700313

First published 2026

A catalogue record for this publication is available from the British Library

A Cataloging-in-Publication data record for this Element is available from the Library of Congress

ISBN 978-1-009-70030-6 Hardback
ISBN 978-1-009-70027-6 Paperback
ISSN 2977-7585 (online)
ISSN 2977-7577 (print)

Middlemen in Search Equilibrium

A Survey

Elements in Money and Banking

DOI: 10.1017/9781009700313
First published online: May 2026

Grace Xun Gong
Zhejiang University

Ziqi Qiao
University of Wisconsin-Madison

Randall Wright
Zhejiang University and Wisconsin School of Business

Author for correspondence: Grace Xun Gong, gracegx1203@outlook.com

Abstract: Surveys the literature on middlemen (i.e., intermediation in exchange), reviewing, extending, and consolidating key developments in the field. This is important because intermediated trade is common in reality but absent in standard general equilibrium theory. The authors focus on research using search theory. In various models, agents may act as middlemen when they are good at search, bargaining, recognizing quality, storing inventories, using credit, etcetera. The theory applies to markets for goods, inputs, or assets. The authors discuss versions with indivisible or divisible goods, fixed or endogenous participation, stationary and dynamic equilibria, and some implications for efficiency and volatility.

Keywords: middlemen, intermediation, search, bargaining, frictions

ISBNs: 9781009700306 (HB), 9781009700276 (PB), 9781009700313 (OC)
ISSNs: 2977-7585 (online), 2977-7577 (print)

Contents

Despite the important role played by intermediation in most markets, it is largely ignored by the standard theoretical literature. This is because a study of intermediation requires a basic model that describes explicitly the trade frictions that give rise to the function of intermediation. But this is missing from the standard market models, where the actual process of trading is left unmodeled.

Rubinstein and Wolinsky (1987)

1 Introduction

This Element surveys the theoretical economic literature on middlemen (i.e., intermediaries in the exchange process). This is relevant because, as is well recognized, intermediation plays a big role in many (if not most) markets for consumption goods, productive inputs, and assets, yet the activity is absent in standard general equilibrium theory. We present modern developments using search theory to study middlemen in markets with explicit frictions. The goal is not to discuss every paper in detail, but to develop a consistent framework that can be used to illustrate various models and ideas.[1]

Starting with Rubinstein and Wolinsky (1987), this research builds models where intermediation emerges because certain agents have comparative advantages along some dimension. A general version of the Rubinstein–Wolinsky model is presented in Section 3, but here is an outline. There are consumers and producers of something called x, plus other agents that neither consume nor produce x, but potentially could act as middlemen by buying it from producers and selling it to consumers. In many (but not all) models agents meet bilaterally at random. In the original formulation, these other agents perform a middleman function when they have an advantage in search (i.e., they meet consumers faster than producers meet consumers).

Further studies generalize the framework's technical specification by allowing different bargaining powers (in the original specification all agents have the same bargaining power); general populations (in the original the measures of buyers and sellers are the same); endogenous entry (participation is fixed in the original); production, search, and storage costs (these are absent from the original model); goods that are divisible (goods are indivisible in the original); and payment frictions (the original has transferable utility).

Further studies also explore different assumptions about the kinds of advantage middlemen might have, including superior information that lets them better recognize quality, a technology that lets them hold larger or more diverse inventories, and a superior ability to better enforce debt repayment. A main goal is to characterize the set of parameters consistent with the existence of equilibria with active intermediaries. Papers also investigate whether there is

[1] Since the literature in the area is large, and growing, we posted an online bibliography that can be updated over time at https://github.com/qiao-ziqi/middlemen.

uniqueness or multiplicity of equilibria, as well as how intermediation affects efficiency. They also analyze if it attenuates or accentuates volatility. Of particular interest is finding conditions under which there emerge different patterns of exchange – only direct trade, only indirect trade, or both. Some papers also consider how multiple middlemen enter into intermediation chains. We review all of these in what follows.

While this Element mainly concerns theory, some facts help the motivation. In an early contribution, Spulber (1996a) documented that intermediated exchange accounted for over 25% of GDP in the US in 1993, including retail trade (9.33%), wholesale trade (6.51%), finance/insurance (7.28%), and selected services (1.89%). Updating this from 1993 to 2025, 25% increased to 35.1% (BEA, US Department of Commerce, Federal Reserve Bank of St. Louis). For food, from 1993 to 2023, the share of dollars going to farmers and manufacturers declined from about 34% to 29%, while the share going to wholesale (distribution), retailing (supermarkets and grocery stores), and food services (restaurants, cafeterias, etc.) rose from 48% to 58% (USDA ERS Food Dollar Series). Switching from food to drink, in 2017 direct-to-consumer wine sales in the US were around 10% of the market, with the rest accounted for by retailers (Rhodes et al. 2021). In real estate, intermediated trade accounts for 91% of sales. In the labor market, recruitment and staffing firms account for two-thirds of all postings and attract most of the applications (Davis and de la Parra 2025).

Philippon (2015) discusses the share of financial intermediation in GDP and how it changes over time. As Lagos and Rocheteau (2006) report, different asset markets feature different microstructures – that is, while intermediated trade in the fed funds market is about 40%, NASDAQ is closer to 100%, and many OTC (over-the-counter) markets are in between, including markets for corporate, municipal, and emerging-market debt. In international trade, the impact of intermediation shows up in various ways, such as the fact that in the US wholesale and retail firms account for approximately 11% and 24% of exports and imports (Bernard et al. 2007). The use of intermediary firms is especially important in developing economies, especially in Asia – for example, in the 1980s 300 trading (nonmanufacturing) Japanese firms accounted for 80% of trade (Rossman 1984).

In China today, Ahn et al. (2011) show 22% of exports are handled by intermediaries. In firm-level data, they also show that small or less productive firms rely disproportionately on intermediaries to access foreign markets. Those firms using intermediaries are significantly more likely to eventually become direct exporters, implying intermediaries lower entry barriers and boost overall trade. In the used-car market, Biglaiser et al. (2020) document that dealer-mediated transactions command a consistent price premium over private sales, especially for older vehicles, and that cars sold through dealers exhibit higher quality. Together, all these findings demonstrate that middlemen can affect both the quantity and the quality of trade, and that suggests they are worth studying seriously.

Monieson (2010) provides historical perspective on middlemen. While there are many interesting facets of this history that could be mentioned, one issue going back a long way is this: Do they provide a useful service, or simply profit from buying low and selling high? An extreme view is epitomized by Benjamin Disraeli, who said "It is well-known what a middleman is: he is a man who bamboozles one party and plunders the other."[2] An alternative possibility is that they facilitate the process of exchange, which can enhance efficiency and welfare. As Ayn Rand (1971, p. 313) put it, "The shortest distance between two points is not a straight line – it's a middleman."[3]

Reality may be somewhere between these extremes. While theory alone does not definitively resolve this debate, modeling intermediated trade formally in economic theory helps us understand the relevant factors. Before getting into formal models, we offer this story from Turner (1836, pp. 115–16), quoting a source from the eleventh century on the practice of buying low and selling high:

> In the Saxon dialogues, the merchant (mancgere) is introduced: "I say that I am useful to the king, and to ealdormen, and to the rich, and to all people. I ascend my ship with my merchandise, and sail over the sea-like places, and sell my things, and buy dear things which are not produced in this land, and I bring them to you here with great danger over the sea; and sometimes I suffer shipwreck, with the loss of all my things, scarcely escaping myself."
> "What things do you bring to us?"
> "Skins, silks, costly gems, and gold; various garments, pigment, wine, oil, ivory, and orichalcus, copper, and tin, silver, glass, and suchlike."
> "Will you sell your things here as you brought them here?"
> "I will not, because what would my labour benefit me? I will sell them dearer here than I bought them there, that I may get some profit, to feed me, my wife, and children."

[2] Speech in the House of Commons (11 April 1845), p. 565. Available at https://api.parliament.uk/historic-hansard/commons/1845/apr/11/maynooth-college#S3V0079P0_18450411_HOC_42

[3] An even more positive perspective comes from the TV series *The Middleman*, where the title character is "a freelance fixer of 'exotic problems', which include mad scientists wanting to take over the world and hostile aliens" (https://en.wikipedia.org/wiki/The_Middleman_(TV_series)). Unfortunately the theory presented below does not include such 'exotic problems' explicitly, but we suggest (with tongue in cheek) that this could be a promising direction for future research.

The rest of the Element is organized as follows. Section 2 presents a rudimentary environment by way of introducing some basic terminology, notation, and ideas. Section 3 extends this to a generalization of the environment in Rubinstein–Wolinsky. Section 4 considers alternative assumptions and analyzes the possibility of multiple equilibria and endogenous dynamics. Sections 5 and 6 discuss information frictions and intermediation chains. Section 7 considers papers on inventories and directed rather than random search, while Section 8 summarizes some work focusing on OTC asset markets. Section 9 focuses on the relationship between middlemen, money, and credit. Section 10 mentions papers that do not fit elsewhere in the Element but are still relevant. Section 11 concludes.

2 A Simple Model

Before discussing the literature, it is useful to construct a simple two-period model that captures some of the main ideas, and, in particular, provides a clean version of the classic result in Rubinstein and Wolinsky (1987). It also lets us introduce notation, labeling, etcetera.

There are three agents – a producer P, a middleman M, and a consumer C – that are interested in trading an indivisible good x. The producer P produces one unit of x at cost c, which we set to zero for now (for some applications it is better to think of P as being endowed with x). The consumer C derives utility $u > c$ from consuming one unit (for some applications it is better to think of x as an input or asset and u as C's profit or return to acquiring it). The middleman M neither produces nor consumes x, but could acquire it from P and resell it to C; that is intermediated trade.

There are two periods, or stages, to the trading process, with C indifferent between getting x in the first or second stage. Trade is bilateral, with the terms of trade determined here by generalized Nash bargaining, where the share of agent i when bargaining with j is denoted θ_{ij}. There is at most one meeting per period, and the probability agent i meets agent j in each period is α_{ij}, or equivalently α_{ji}, by the bilateral nature of meetings. For now the α's are parameters; later, they come from an underlying meeting technology. If P meets C in the first stage, they trade, and the game is over. What is to be determined: Do P and M trade if they meet in the first stage?

Let there be returns to holding x for P and M in the second stage, denoted ρ_p and ρ_m, where $\rho_j < 0$ stands for storage costs in goods markets, while $\rho_j > 0$ stands for dividends in asset markets. For now we assume $\rho_j < 0$ (but see Section 4), with the cost incurred between the first and second stage, so it is sunk when P or M with x meets C in stage 2. In addition to x, there is a second tradable object, y, that is divisible and serves as a payment instrument. The most generous way to think about this is the following: Any agent can produce or consume y at constant marginal cost, or constant marginal utility, both normalized to 1, and when i acquires x from j, the former makes a payment y_{ji} that increases j's payoff and decreases i's payoff by the same amount.

This way of sharing the trade surplus, using y as a means of payment, is essentially what is usually called *transferable utility*. Our interpretation is generous in the sense that the direct transfer of utility is problematic. Consider Binmore (1992):

> Sometimes it is assumed that contracts can be written that specify that some utils are to be transferred from one player to another... Alert readers will be suspicious about such transfers... Utils are not real objects and so cannot really be transferred; only physical commodities can actually be exchanged. Transferable utility therefore only makes proper sense in special cases. The leading case is that in which both players are risk-neutral and their von Neumann and Morgenstern utility scales have been chosen so that their utility from a sum of money x [in our notation, y] is simply $U(x) = x$ [in our notation, $U(y) = y$]. Transferring one util from one player to another is then just the same as transferring one dollar.

We agree that "Utils are not real objects and so cannot really be transferred," although we are less sure that "only physical commodities can actually be exchanged" since it seems clear that, for example, information or ideas can also be exchanged. A bigger issue concerns the claim that transferable utility is the same as paying with money. In serious monetary models, agents have a value function, or indirect utility function, over money holdings, but it is not generally linear (see surveys by Lagos et al. 2017 and Rocheteau and Nosal 2017). Well, in some models, sometimes money actually does enter linearly but *up to a point*, which does *not* correspond to transferable utility for the simple reason that buyers tend to run out of money, while in transferable utility models they never run out of utils.

Therefore, instead of pretending that y is money, it is better to say there is a good y that anyone can consume and produce. This avoids Binmore's justified complaint about utils being transferred without doing a disservice to monetary/payment economics. At the risk of sounding pedantic, we emphasize this because work in the area is concerned with microfoundations, so it is important to think through such details, although we try not to dwell on it too much in what follows.

So, when x changes hands, C pays y_{pc} to P, C pays y_{mc} to M, and M pays y_{pm} to P. Interpreting these as prices, we call y_{pc} the *direct price*, y_{pm} the *wholesale price*, and y_{mc} the *retail price*. However, this is not as obvious as it may appear. First, if x is divisible, and endogenous, as it is in some of the models presented in Sections 5, 7, and 9, in principle it might be better to call y_{ij}/x_{ij} the price. Having said that, in practice it could be that we see (in the data) y_{ij} but not x_{ij}, which is especially relevant when x corresponds to quality rather than quantity. Second, while y_{ij}/x_{ij} is the price of x in terms of y, it makes as much sense to say x_{ij}/y_{ij} is the price of y in terms of x.

In standard usage *the* price refers to the amount of money a buyer pays to get x, which is hard to understand in models without money. Indeed, without money changing hands, it is not at all clear who is the buyer and who is the seller, any more than those labels make sense when i gives j apples in trade for bananas. This may or may not matter, depending on context (see Wright and Wong 2014 for an extended discussion). In any case, if we call the ys prices, there arise several other interesting variables, like the spread $y_{mc} - y_{pm}$ and markup y_{mc}/y_{pm}.

In the first period, P is assumed to produce x before meetings occur. If P meets C they always trade, as mentioned. If P meets no one, or P meets M and they decide not to trade, P and C proceed to stage 2, while M is assumed to drop out, which, by assumption, does not affect the probability P and C meet. If P meets M and they trade, M and C proceed to stage 2 while P drops out, since, by assumption, P can only produce once here. Note that in a stage 1 meeting, P and M can differ along three dimensions: α_{ic}, their probability of meeting C in stage 2; θ_{ic}, their bargaining power; and ρ_i, their return to holding x, which for the purposes of this discussion satisfies $\rho_i \leq 0$ (but see Section 4).

Let V_p, V_m, and V_c be the value functions of P, M, and C in the second stage. Then, the surpluses S_{ij} when i trades with j, using the labels direct, retail, and wholesale suggested earlier, are:

$$S_{cp} = u - y_{pc} \text{ and } S_{pc} = y_{pc}, \tag{1}$$

$$S_{cm} = u - y_{mc} \text{ and } S_{mc} = y_{mc}, \tag{2}$$

$$S_{mp} = V_m - y_{pm} \text{ and } S_{pm} = y_{pm} - V_p. \tag{3}$$

In each trade y solves the bargaining problem

$$y_{ij} = \arg\max_y S_{ij}(y)^{\theta_{ij}} S_{ji}(y)^{\theta_{ji}}. \tag{4}$$

However, with transferable utility (in the sense discussed earlier, where i produces and j consumes it with equal marginal cost and utility), the bargaining protocol, as long as it is reasonable, does not matter. So, we simply say i gets a share θ_{ij} of total surplus $S_{ij} + S_{ji}$, which leads to

$$y_{pc} = \theta_{pc}u, \; y_{mc} = \theta_{mc}u \text{ and } y_{pm} = \theta_{pm}V_m + \theta_{mp}V_p. \tag{5}$$

Let the probability P and M trade at stage 1 be τ. Then the second-stage value functions are

$$V_c = (1-\tau)\alpha_{cp}S_{cp} + \tau\alpha_{cm}S_{cm}, \tag{6}$$

$$V_p = \alpha_{pc}S_{pc} + \rho_p, \tag{7}$$

$$V_m = \alpha_{mc}S_{mc} + \rho_m. \tag{8}$$

In other words, these values are the product of meeting probabilities and surpluses, minus storage cost. Note that for now it is taken for granted that all agents participate in the market, but that will be checked in Section 3.

Then, after inserting the Ss and ys, we have

$$V_c = (1-\tau)\alpha_{cp}\theta_{cp}u + \tau\alpha_{cm}\theta_{cm}u, \tag{9}$$

$$V_p = \alpha_{pc}\theta_{pc}u + \rho_p, \tag{10}$$

$$V_m = \alpha_{mc}\theta_{mc}u + \rho_m. \tag{11}$$

Note that P and M do not enter the second stage simultaneously. At least one of V_p or V_m is an off-equilibrium value. Nonetheless, we need to track both in order to determine τ, the probability of wholesale trade. Here τ only depends on the sign of the total surplus $S_{mp} + S_{pm}$; that is, whether there are gains from trade between P and M. What we call the best response conditions are then:

$$\tau = \begin{cases} 1 & \text{if } V_m > V_p \\ [0,1] & \text{if } V_m = V_p \\ 0 & \text{if } V_m < V_p \end{cases}. \tag{12}$$

When all agents participate, τ is the only decision. Thus, an *equilibrium* is given by V's and τ satisfying (9)–(12), from which other variables, like the ys, are easily determined.

Figure 1 shows the structure of the model. It is easy to see that equilibrium exists and is unique. Letting $\Gamma = \alpha_{mc}\theta_{mc} + \rho_m/u - \alpha_{pc}\theta_{pc} - \rho_p/u$, in equilibrium $\tau = 1$ if $\Gamma > 0$ and $\tau = 0$ if $\Gamma < 0$.[4] Intuitively, $\tau = 1$ means M is active, intermediating by buying x from P and selling it to C, if and only if M has some advantage over P. This in general means M has some combination of being better at search, $\alpha_{mc} > \alpha_{pc}$, or bargaining, $\theta_{mc} > \theta_{pc}$, or storage, $\rho_m > \rho_p$. Although their environment is more complicated in some ways, Rubinstein–Wolinsky (1987) is, in our notation, the special case where $\rho_p = \rho_m$ and $\theta_{pc} = \theta_{mc}$, which gives their classic result: M is active if and only if $\alpha_{mc} > \alpha_{pc}$. More generally, M can be fundamentally inferior to P in terms of search or storage, $\alpha_{mc} < \alpha_{pc}$ or $\rho_m < \rho_p$, and equilibrium can still

4 We ignore $\Gamma = 0$, where any $\tau \in [0, 1]$ satisfies the equilibrium conditions, since that holds on a set of measure 0 in parameter space.

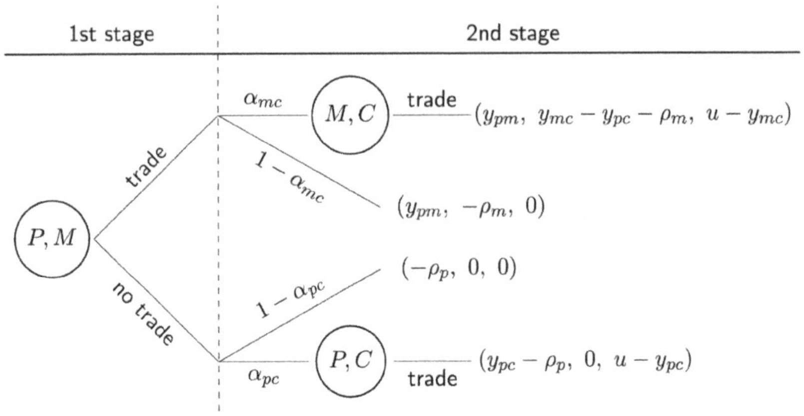

Figure 1 Structure of the simple model.

have $\tau = 1$, if M has an advantage over P squeezing surplus out of C, which looks like inefficient rent-seeking activity.

To be precise, we can measure welfare by the sum of the Vs, which equals the expected utility of C minus the cost of P or M delivering the goods. The optimal wholesale trade maximizes welfare:

$$\tau^* = \arg\max_{\tau} (1-\tau)\left(\alpha_{pc}u + \rho_p\right) + \tau\left(\alpha_{mc}u + \rho_m\right).$$

Letting $\Gamma^* = \alpha_{mc} + \rho_m/u - \alpha_{pc} - \rho_p/u$, it follows that $\tau^* = 1$ if $\Gamma^* > 0$ and $\tau^* = 0$ otherwise. Note that Γ depends on the θ_{ic}s while Γ^* does not. Given Γ and Γ^*, we can evaluate when equilibrium is efficient. In the special Rubinstein–Wolinsky (1987) case, $\rho_p = \rho_m$ and $\theta_{pc} = \theta_{mc}$, equilibrium and efficiency coincide: Both imply middlemen should be active if and only if $\alpha_{mc} > \alpha_{pc}$. However, going beyond their special case, we can have $\tau = 1$ when $\tau^* = 0$ or vice versa, depending on parameters, and in particular depending on the θs.[5]

The aforementioned analysis is predicated on P and M participating in the market, which must be checked. For stage 1, everyone participates, since it is costless. For stage 2, while C still participates for free, for $j = P, M$ we need $V_j \geq 0$, or, in terms of primitives, $\alpha_{jc}\theta_{jc}u \geq -\rho_j$. In general, there are four possibilities for the equilibrium pattern of exchange, or what we call the

[5] If $\rho_p = \rho_m$, the equilibrium is efficient for any values of the α_{ic}s if and only if $\theta_{mc} = \theta_{pc}$, i.e., bargaining power does not distort the trading probability. If $\rho_p \neq \rho_m$, the equilibrium is efficient if and only if $\alpha_{cm}\theta_{cm} = \alpha_{cp}\theta_{cp}$, which implies that C is indifferent between trading with P or M ex ante, and thus the private incentive to maximize $S_{mp} + S_{pm}$ aligns with the social optimum. More discussion of these matters appears in Sections 3 and 9.

equilibrium *regime*, in stage 2: Regime N, for *no* trade, occurs if $\alpha_{jc}\theta_{jc}u < -\rho_j$ for both $j = P, M$, so expected profit does not justify the cost. Regime D, for *direct* trade, occurs if $\alpha_{jc}\theta_{jc}u \geq -\rho_j$ for P but not M. Regime I, for *indirect* trade only, occurs if $\alpha_{jc}\theta_{jc}u \geq -\rho_j$ for M but not P. Regime B, for *both* direct and indirect trade, occurs if $\alpha_{jc}\theta_{jc}u \geq -\rho_j$ for P and M. These four regimes appear in several other models discussed in Sections 4, 5, 6, and 9.

Equilibrium features a classic holdup problem since the search/storage cost is sunk when P or M meets C at stage 2. Likewise, the wholesale price y_{pm} at which M gets x from P in stage 1 is sunk when M meets C. Agents cannot recoup sunk costs in bargaining for the usual reason: These costs are paid whether or not they trade, so they cancel out of the surplus (the payoff to trade minus the payoff to no trade). This distorts equilibrium as follows: In equilibrium M and P participate as stage 2 sellers when $\alpha_{jc}\theta_{jc}u \geq -\rho_j$, while efficiency suggests they should participate when $\alpha_{jc}u \geq -\rho_j$. For the equilibrium and efficiency conditions to coincide for all values of the parameters we need $\theta_{ij} = 1$.[6]

Holdup problems exist in many economic models with bargaining. One take on this is that they can be avoided by having agents contract the terms of trade before incurring sunk costs. That is sometimes ruled out exogenously. In search theory, ruling it out seems less ad hoc once one recognizes that you cannot contract with someone before you contact them. We can eliminate part of the problem by an assumption on exogenous parameters, $\rho_j = 0$, but the endogenous wholesale price y_{pm} is still sunk when M and C meet. Rubinstein and Wolinsky (1987) propose a *consignment* procedure to deal with that: M only pays P after C pays M. Whether this is feasible depends on assumptions – can P and M stay in contact while waiting for C? In any case, it does not affect their main result: Given $\theta_{mc} = \theta_{pc}$ and $\rho_{mc} = \rho_{pc}$, activity by M depends solely on the sign of $\alpha_{mc} - \alpha_{pc}$.

In what follows we consider other advantages middlemen may have. We also consider going beyond two periods, sometimes to an infinite horizon, which is interesting and even crucial in some applications (e.g., introducing money or endogenous debt limits). A goal is to characterize the equilibrium set to see when we can support different regimes. Another is to discuss existence, uniqueness or multiplicity, and dynamics in various extensions of the basic framework.

6 For aficionados of search theory, this is related to the Hosios condition and Mortensen rule for the efficiency of equilibrium with search and bargaining (see, e.g., Gong 2018 for a discussion in the context of middleman models).

3 Extending the Simple Model

We now present (a generalized version of) the framework used in Rubinstein and Wolinsky (1987). Time t is continuous and the horizon is infinite. A continuum of agents come in three types, P, C, and M, acting in the roles played in Section 2. They all discount future payoffs at rate r. While different versions presented in this section make different assumptions about this, in the original specification type M stay in the market forever while P and C exit after one trade, with an exogenous inflow of new P and C agents so the market can be open in the long run.[7]

At any t the state of the system is given by the distribution of inventories across type M. With x indivisible, an individual M has inventory $I \in \{0,1,\ldots,\hat{I}\}$, where $\hat{I}$ may be finite or infinite. Many papers (though not all) set $\hat{I} = 1$, so there are just two kinds of middlemen; let us call them M_1 and M_0, with the subscript indicating inventory. Hence, at any t a measure N_1 are type M_1 with 1 unit of x, and a measure N_0 are type M_0 with 0 inventory, where $N_0 + N_1 = N_m$. Restricting $I \in \{0,1\}$ is a technological assumption that M can store at most one unit of x, and P can produce and C can consume at most one unit at a time. This assumption has precedent in search theory,[8] and Section 7 discusses papers that relax it.

Given $I \in \{0,1\}$, the return to $i = P, M$ from holding a unit of x is again ρ_i. We can also add a fixed entry cost κ_i for type i, different from ρ_i in that it is paid once and not each period, but $\kappa_i = 0$ for now. Meetings are characterized by Poisson processes with arrival rates α_{ij} denoting the probability per unit time that type i meets j, and bilateral meetings imply the identities $N_i\alpha_{ij} = N_j\alpha_{ji}$.

The meeting process in Rubinstein–Wolinsky can be interpreted in terms of spatial separation, even if they were not specific about it. A significant feature of their formulation is that the measure of type i does not affect the probability j meets k when $j \neq i$ and $k \neq i$. Other papers proceed differently, and a common specification has the probability that i meets j proportional to the fraction of

[7] Some formulations in Sections 3, 4, 8, and 9 have P and C in the market forever and fix the measure of type i at N_i. Others have costly entry for some types so the population is endogenous. Still others allow some agents to choose their type, e.g., those that are not type C can choose to act as P or M. Sometimes these different environments differ in tractability or in substantive results, but it is a virtue of the framework that it can accommodate diverse assumptions.

[8] Restrictions similar to $I \in \{0,1\}$ are featured in search papers going back to classics such as Diamond (1982), monetary models following Kiyotaki and Wright (1989), banking models like Cavalcanti and Wallace (1999), and OTC financial market models like Duffie et al. (2005). It is also similar to specifications where firms can hire just one worker in labor models, like Pissarides (2000), or agents want just one partner in relationship models, like Burdett and Coles (1997). These are all useful contributions even if $\{0,1\}$ restrictions are unrealistic and can be relaxed, but usually at a substantial cost in terms of complexity.

type j among the total population of participating agents in the market. This is sometimes called uniform random meetings, and implies the measure of M in the market, for example, affects the probability P meets C, which can be understood as a congestion effect that is assumed away in the original model.

Let τ_{ij} be the probability of trade when i meets j. With transferable utility, as described earlier, i wants to trade with j if and only if j wants to trade with i if and only if the joint surplus is positive, so we can use either τ_{ij} or τ_{ji} to indicate the probability they trade. Some of the τs are trivial; for example, $\tau_{c0} = \tau_{p1} = 0$ is automatic since when C meets M with inventory 0, or P meets M with inventory 1, trade is impossible. The rate at which M switches from M_1 to M_0 is $\alpha_{1c}\tau_{1c}$, and the rate at which M switches back is $\alpha_{0p}\tau_{0p}$. In general, both are the product of chance (a meeting) and choice (a trade).

Let V_p and V_c be the value functions for P and C, and let V_0 or V_1 be the value functions for M holding 0 or 1 unit of x. As mentioned, here C and P leave after trading while M stays. The surplus S_{ij} when i trades with j is:

$$S_{cp} = u - y_{pc} - V_c \text{ and } S_{pc} = y_{pc} - c - V_p, \tag{13}$$

$$S_{cm} = u - y_{mc} - V_c \text{ and } S_{mc} = y_{mc} - V_1 + V_0, \tag{14}$$

$$S_{mp} = V_1 - V_0 - y_{pm} \text{ and } S_{pm} = y_{pm} - c - V_p, \tag{15}$$

where P is assumed to produce upon meeting as in Rubinstein–Wolinsky.

For the terms of trade, with transferable utility, reasonable bargaining solutions all give similar results. Here we use generalized Nash bargaining: In each trade, the payment y solves

$$y_{ij} = \arg\max_{y} S_{ij}(y)^{\theta_{ij}} S_{ji}(y)^{\theta_{ji}}. \tag{16}$$

This yields:

$$y_{pc} = \theta_{pc}(u - V_c) + \theta_{cp}\left(c + V_p\right), \tag{17}$$

$$y_{mc} = \theta_{mc}(u - V_c) + \theta_{cm}(V_1 - V_0), \tag{18}$$

$$y_{pm} = \theta_{pm}(V_1 - V_0) + \theta_{mp}\left(c + V_p\right). \tag{19}$$

Thus, payment y is a weighted average of the benefit to the agent receiving x and the cost to the agent giving it up; for example, when C gets x from M the benefit to the former is $u - V_c$ while the cost for the latter is $V_1 - V_0$.

Also, with transferable utility, the best response conditions for whether i and j trade are given by:

$$\tau_{ij} = \begin{cases} 1 & \text{if } S_{ij} + S_{ji} > 0 \\ [0,1] & \text{if } S_{ij} + S_{ji} = 0 \\ 0 & \text{if } S_{ij} + S_{ji} < 0 \end{cases}. \tag{20}$$

The original Rubinstein–Wolinsky setup has new C and P agents flowing into the market at an exogenous rate E, making the stocks N_c and N_p endogenous. The stocks N_1 and N_0 are also endogenous, but of course we only need to keep track of N_1 since $N_0 = N_m - N_1$ with N_m fixed. Hence, the relevant laws of motion or the state of the system are

$$\dot{N}_c = E - \left(\alpha_{cp} + \alpha_{c1}\right) N_c, \tag{21}$$

$$\dot{N}_p = E - \left(\alpha_{pc} + \alpha_{p0}\right) N_p, \tag{22}$$

$$\dot{N}_1 = \left(N_m - N_1\right) \alpha_{0p} \tau_{mp} - N_1 \alpha_{1c} \tau_{mc}, \tag{23}$$

where the $\dot{N}$s are derivatives with respect to time.

The value functions expressed in terms of S_{ij} satisfy

$$rV_c = \alpha_{cp} \tau_{cp} S_{cp} + \alpha_{c1} \tau_{c1} S_{cm} + \dot{V}_c, \tag{24}$$

$$rV_p = \alpha_{pc} \tau_{pc} S_{pc} + \alpha_{p0} \tau_{p0} S_{pm} + \rho_p + \dot{V}_p, \tag{25}$$

$$rV_1 = \alpha_{1c} \tau_{1c} S_{mc} + \rho_m + \dot{V}_1, \tag{26}$$

$$rV_0 = \alpha_{0p} \tau_{0p} S_{mp} + \dot{V}_0. \tag{27}$$

Consider (24). In words, it says the flow value rV_c is the rate α_{cp} at which C meets P, times the probability τ_{cp} they trade, times C's surplus from that trade; plus the rate α_{c1} at which C meets M with inventory, times the probability τ_{c1} they trade, times C's surplus from that trade; plus the pure rate of time change $\dot{V}_c$, which is 0 in steady state but not in general. The other equations have similar interpretations.

With dynamic models we have to be a little more careful in defining things. An *equilibrium* here consists of paths for: the value functions $\mathbf{V} = \left(V_p, V_c, V_0, V_1\right)$, the terms of trade, which with x indivisible are given by $\mathbf{y} = \left(y_{pc}, y_{pm}, y_{mc}\right)$, the trading strategies $\boldsymbol{\tau} = \left(\tau_{pc}, \tau_{p0}, \tau_{1c}\right)$, and the state variables $\mathbf{N} = \left(N_c, N_p, N_1\right)$, satisfying the dynamic programming equations, bargaining solutions, best response conditions, and laws of motion. Equilibrium must also satisfy an initial condition saying where the system starts in terms of N, plus the usual nonnegativity and boundedness conditions.[9] A *stationary equilibrium* is a special case where $\mathbf{V}$, $\mathbf{y}$, and $\boldsymbol{\tau}$ are time-invariant functions of $\mathbf{N}$ (they can depend on the state but not the date). A steady state is a solution to the equilibrium conditions other than the initial condition where endogenous variables are constant.

[9] Boundedness can be interpreted as a transversality condition necessary for individual optimization, or simply a feasibility condition (payoffs cannot go to ∞). See Rocheteau and Wright (2013), e.g., for a formal discussion in the context of related models.

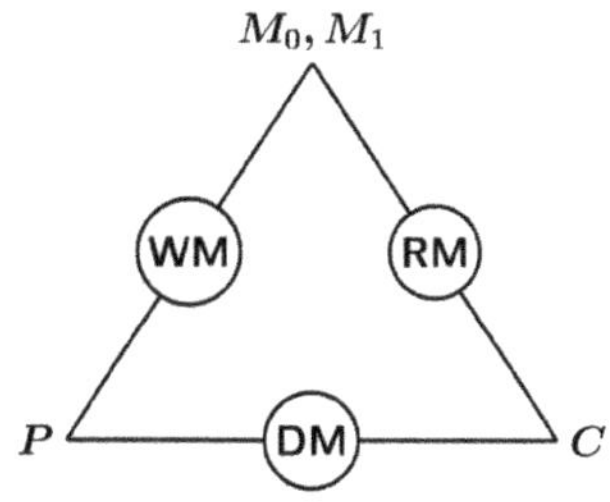

Figure 2 Market structure consistent with Rubinstein–Wolinsky (1987).

In Rubinstein–Wolinsky, as mentioned earlier, the arrival rate α_{ij} depends on N_i and N_j, the measures of i and j, but not on other Ns. This rules out third-party congestion in the meeting process, which is convenient, but the microfoundations may not be obvious. Figure 2 depicts a market structure consistent with their assumptions, featuring spatial separation, as in Gong et al. (2024).

In Figure 2 different types are located at distinct locations represented by nodes on a triangle. Agents visit both of their nearby markets, represented by the edges, but not the third – it's just too far. One can interpret this as saying there are three submarkets labeled as follows: a direct market (DM) with C and P; a wholesale market (WM) with P and M_0; and a retail market (RM) with M_1 and C. This spatial separation is consistent with the Rubinstein–Wolinsky paper.

Now is a good time to discuss meeting technologies. Following textbook methods (e.g., Pissarides 2000), consider a two-sided market with measures N_b of buyers and N_s of sellers. The number of meetings is assumed to be an increasing, concave function $\mu(N_b, Ns)$, implying arrival rates $\alpha_i = \mu(N_b, Ns)/N_i$. A common assumption that we adopt is that μ displays constant returns to scale, which implies the arrival rates depend only on market tightness, N_b/N_s. As mentioned earlier, and as Figure 2 shows, agents participate in both of their nearby markets but not the third.[10]

This allows us to use a general two-sided meeting technology in each of the submarkets, which is convenient because it is not clear how to use a general meeting technology in a three-sided market (more on this in Sections 4, 6, 8, and 9). To proceed, let the DM, WM, and RM meetings technologies be $\phi_j \mu(\cdot)$, for $j = D, W, R$, where the ϕs are constants describing search efficiency. Then, as in Rubinstein–Wolinsky, assume $\phi_W = \phi_R$, but ϕ_D can be different, and in

[10] An interpretation consistent with this is that there are two-person households, and one member goes to each of the nearby markets (similar to the use of worker–shopper pairs in Lucas 1980, or the even larger families in Shi 1997). One can also think of it in terms of a telephone technology, as Mortensen and Pissarides (1999) evoke in their search models, where for our purposes long-distance calls are prohibitively expensive.

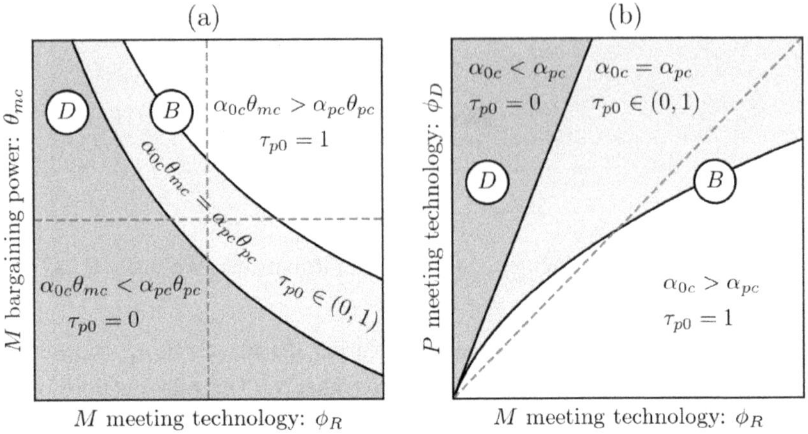

Figure 3 Equilibrium set as a function of parameters.

particular M is better than P at meeting C based on the fundamental technology when $\phi_R > \phi_D$, although the equilibrium arrival rates depend on tightness.

Now, as in Rubinstein–Wolinsky, we focus on steady states that are symmetric in the sense that $N_p = N_c$, which implies $N_1 = N_0$, $\alpha_{cp} = \alpha_{pc}$, $\alpha_{c1} = \alpha_{p0}$, and $\alpha_{1c} = \alpha_{0p}$. Also, as in their original model, we set $c = \rho_p = \rho_m = 0$. The goal is to determine the trading pattern given by the τs. It is clear that C and P always trade ($\tau_{cp} = \tau_{pc} = 1$). The more interesting questions are whether M without inventory trade with P (determined by $\tau_{p0} = \tau_{0p}$), and whether M with inventory trade with C (determined by $\tau_{1c} = \tau_{c1}$). Clearly, if $\tau_{p0} = 1$ then $\tau_{1c} = 1$, since a buy-and-hold strategy for M is not a good idea when $\rho_m = 0$. What remains to determine is whether M and P trade, as determined by τ_{mc}.

Although the Rubinstein–Wolinsky paper does not mention existence or uniqueness, from Gong et al. (2024) we know that a symmetric steady state exists and is unique. This is illustrated in Figure 3. In the panel (a), on the vertical axis is M's bargaining power, with the horizontal dashed line giving P's bargaining power, so that above the line M is better than P at extracting surplus from C. On the horizontal axis is M's search efficiency, defined by ϕ_R in meeting technology, $\phi_R \mu(\cdot)$, while the vertical dashed line represents $\phi_R = \phi_D$–so to the right of this line M has a fundamental advantage in search. Panel (b) is similar but drawn in ϕ space.

Figure 3 shows there are regions of parameter space where M and P trade with probability $\tau_{p0} = 1$, where they trade with probability $\tau_{p0} = 0$, and where they trade with probability $\tau_{p0} \in (0,1)$. In terms of the language introduced earlier, there are two possible outcomes: Regime D or B emerges when $\tau_{p0} = 0$ or $\tau_{p0} > 0$. (Regimes N and I for now cannot emerge because P is always in the market and happy to trade with C for now – but see Sections 4 and 9) Related to Section 2, the result can be stated as follows: $\alpha_{1c}\theta_{mc} > \alpha_{pc}\theta_{pc}$ implies $\tau_{p0} = 1$, so P and M trade whenever they meet; $\alpha_{1c}\theta_{mc} < \alpha_{pc}\theta_{pc}$ implies P and M never trade when they meet; and $\alpha_{1c}\theta_{mc} = \alpha_{pc}\theta_{pc}$ implies they sometimes trade when they meet.[11]

This is a generalization of the Rubinstein–Wolinsky result, but as intuitive as it may be, the result is not totally satisfactory because it gives a relationship between the αs and τs, both of which are equilibrium outcomes. Hence, it must be interpreted carefully. In particular, it is possible for M to face a less efficient meeting technology, in the sense that ϕ_m is low, but due to endogenous tightness α_{mc} can still be high and hence M still active. Indeed, as panel (a) of Figure 3 shows, M is active when M and P have *the same* meeting technology and bargaining power, at the intersection of the two dashed lines, so by continuity M is active with a moderate disadvantage in their meetings and bargaining. Similarly, M might have a better ϕ and better θ than P, yet $\tau_{p0} < 1$.

So while the result is correct, it could easily be misinterpreted. However, the bigger point is that we now have a characterization of the αs and τs in terms of parameters, as shown in Figure 3. In other words, there is a relationship between the αs and τs, but it is not causal, since both are functions of other, more fundamental, factors.

Having made that point, beyond characterizing M's activity, the theory has implications for how the terms of trade depend on fundamentals. One can check that both y_{pc} and y_{mc} decrease with an improvement in the meeting technology indexed by the ϕs, which seems natural. However, the average y paid by C is nonmonotone because of composition effects – namely, faster search encourages participation by M, and since M charges more than P, the average price paid by C might increase. One can also check that price dispersion (as measured by, e.g., the coefficient of variation) can be nonmonotone.[12]

---

[11] In Section 2 we ignored the case $\alpha_{1c}\theta_{mc} = \alpha_{pc}\theta_{pc}$ because it occurs on a set of measure 0 in parameter space when the arrival rates are exogenous. Here the αs are endogenous, so the unique equilibrium can be one where $\alpha_{1c}\theta_{mc} = \alpha_{pc}\theta_{pc}$ endogenously.

[12] The message here is that in, general, search theory does *not* predict average prices or that price dispersion must fall with reductions in frictions. This is relevant in light of, e.g., Ellison and Ellison (2005, p. 153), who say "evidence from the Internet . . . challenged the existing search models, because we did not see the tremendous decrease in prices and price dispersion that many had predicted," or Baye et al. (2006, p. 324), who say "Reductions in information costs over the past century have neither reduced nor eliminated the levels of price dispersion." In these and other models, improvements in search do not generally lead to lower average prices or price dispersion, as can be seen, e.g., even in the relatively simple model of Burdett and Judd (1983). Moreover, prices need not go down with reductions in search frictions in monetary models, since lower frictions imply buyers carry more money, which allows sellers to charge more (Bethune et al. 2020).

We close this part of the discussion with an important modeling detail. The original Rubinstein–Wolinsky formulation has long-lived M (they stay in the market forever) but short-lived P and C (they leave after one trade), with an exogenous inflow E of the short-lived types. Consider an environment that is similar except C and P, as well as M, stay forever, and in the interest of stationarity set $E = 0$. This makes the surpluses simpler because continuation values cancel with threat points,

$$S_{cp} = u - y_{pc},\ S_{pc} = y_{pc} - c,\ S_{cm} = u - y_{mc},\ \text{and}\ S_{pm} = y_{pm} - c, \tag{28}$$

and the payments become

$$y_{pc} = \theta_{pc}u + \theta_{cp}c, \tag{29}$$

$$y_{mc} = \theta_{mc}u + \theta_{cm}(V_1 - V_0), \tag{30}$$

$$y_{pm} = \theta_{pm}(V_1 - V_0) + \theta_{mp}c. \tag{31}$$

Having all agents in the market forever has consequences. If, for example, type P agents leave after trading, when they meet M they may pass on trade to wait for a meeting with C; but if type P stays after trading, at least with $c = \rho_p = \rho_m = 0$, we must have $\tau_{pm} = 1$, allowing us to shift the focus elsewhere, like endogenous entry. Due to its relative tractability, several models presented herein have all agents in the market forever. A general point that one should always keep in mind is that modeling details like this can matter when exploring microfoundations.[13]

4 Multiplicity and Dynamics

Some papers are concerned with whether we get uniqueness or multiplicity of steady state, and whether there are dynamic equilibria with fluctuations based solely on beliefs. This issue is obviously related to the venerable notion that intermediation, perhaps especially financial intermediation, might engender instability or volatility.[14] Now models based on Rubinstein–Wolinsky have dynamics: If the initial condition for **N** is not at its steady state value, then the unique equilibrium is stationary and converges to steady state, so there is no instability or volatility. What happens if we deviate from the original formulation?

13 Nosal et al. (2015) have a version where each type i exits after trade with probability ς_i, but instead of exogenous inflows, exiting agents are replaced by "clones" (as is known to be more tractable in search models from, e.g., Burdett and Coles 1997). Also, note that whether P and M exit or stay after trade can matter for some issues, but often it does not matter for C, since in many of these models they are more or less mechanical.

14 While much of the literature on the instability/volatility of financial institutions focuses on banks, following Diamond and Dybvig (1983), the issues apply to intermediation more generally. See Gu et al. (2023) and references therein for more discussion.

Nosal et al. (2019) study a three-sided market where P, M, and C interact via a uniform random meeting specification: conditional on i meeting someone, the probability it is type j is proportional to the fraction of type j in the market. Normalizing $N_p + N_c + N_m = 1$, the rate at which type i meets j is $\alpha_{ij} = \alpha N_j$, where α is a baseline arrival rate that is the same for all agents. Notice that rules out something that was the focus of the above analysis: It means $\alpha_{mc} = \alpha_{pc}$ and therefore M cannot have an advantage over P in finding type C.[15]

Even without an advantage in finding type C, M can still be active for other reasons in Nosal et al. (2019). In that paper, all agents stay in the market forever, which, as mentioned earlier, means that P always trades with M since there is no opportunity cost. This might suggest that M agents are doing something socially valuable: When P trades x to M they both become sellers, increasing the probability C gets x. However, rather than having agents acting as M to exploit this idea, it might be better to have them act as P, because the best M can do is to give x to C if M has it in its inventory, while P can give x to C whenever they meet. To pursue this, Nosal et al. (2019) incorporate occupational choice: Anyone who is not type C can choose to act as P or M, or to opt out of the market entirely.

That paper also plays up the distinction between markets for goods and markets for assets by identifying the former with $\rho_j < 0$ and the latter with $\rho_j > 0$ (although that is less relevant given an extension discussed later in this section). It is further assumed that P produces a new unit of x immediately after trading, before the next meeting, as opposed to producing in a meeting. Hence, P as well as M agents carry inventory. It is useful to have inventories depreciate – that is, vanish – at rate δ_j. Thus, a fundamental advantage for M could be captured by $\rho_m > \rho_p$ or $\delta_m < \delta_p$, although for simplicity we set $\delta_j = 0$.

Let us start with $\rho_j < 0$. Focusing for now on steady state, there are three possible outcomes: Regime N, where the market shuts down; Regime D, where the market is open but no one chooses to act as M, so there is only direct trade; and Regime B, where some agents choose to act as M, so there is both direct and indirect trade. (Regime I is ruled out here because M can only be active if some agents act as P, since M gets inventory from P.) It can be shown that equilibrium exists uniquely: There is a unique steady state, and if we start away from steady state there is a unique transition path converging to it.

[15] This needs qualification. The usual specification of uniform random meetings has i meeting j with probability $\alpha_{ij} = \alpha_i N_j$, where $\alpha_i = \alpha$ is the same for all i. That is sufficient but not necessary to satisfy the identities $N_i \alpha_{ij} = N_j \alpha_{ji}$. In general, beyond uniform random meetings, agents may have type-specific meeting rates that confer meeting advantages.

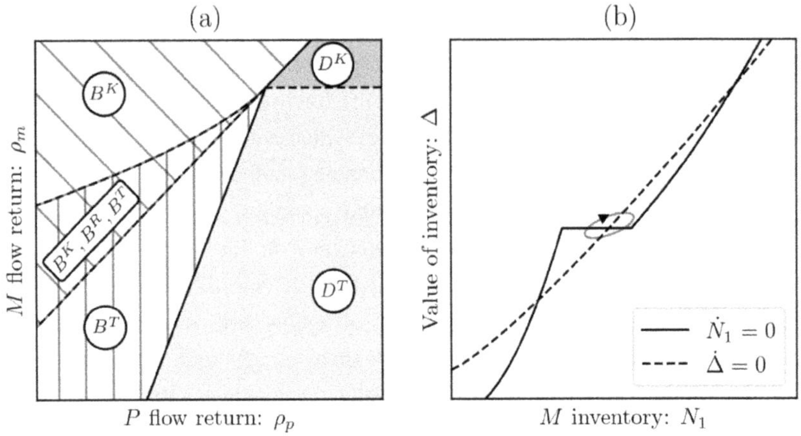

Figure 4 Multiplicity and dynamics.

To give more detail, consider parameter space summarized by storage costs $(-\rho_p, -\rho_m)$ of P and M. It partitions into three regions: When $|\rho_j|$ is big for both $j = P, M$, Regime N emerges, since storage costs are too high to make participation in the market worthwhile; when $|\rho_p|$ is below a threshold and $|\rho_m|$ above a (generally different) threshold, Regime D emerges; and when $|\rho_p|$ is somewhat higher and $|\rho_m|$ lower, Regime B emerges with both direct and indirect trade.

Now consider $\rho_j > 0$. This turns out to be rather different. First, Regime N cannot emerge for a production cost $c = 0$, or, more generally, for any c that is not too big, since P can always produce and hoard x for its return ρ_p. Therefore P must produce, and when P meets C they must trade, since P can produce again. The possible outcomes are shown in panel (a) of Figure 4.[16]

In the graph, there are steady states with $N_m = 0$, which is labeled as region D^K or D^T, where D indicates direct trade and the superscript indicates what happens off the equilibrium path: If there were a type M with x, superscript T says M would trade it to C, while superscript K says M would keep it (while these are the same on the equilibrium path, to show it is an equilibrium, as usual one has to know what happens off the equilibrium path).

Now consider steady states with $N_m > 0$. These are labeled B^T, B^K, and B^R, where the B indicates there is both direct and indirect trade, and the superscripts mean this: T says M trades x to C; K says M keeps x; and R says M randomizes.

[16] Some details concerning panel (b) will be clarified later in this section. Also, note that this model can be used to make various points other than those emphasized here – e.g., for some parameters middlemen are *essential*: the market can open with M active, but if intermediation were to be eliminated – say, by regulation or taxation – it would shut down. See Nosal et al. (2019) for more discussion of welfare and the effects of various parameters.

Naturally, B^K obtains when ρ_m is big and B^T obtains when ρ_m is small. What is interesting is that over some range, where ρ_m is neither too big nor too small, there is multiplicity: two steady states coexist in pure strategies, one with $\tau_{mc} = 0$ and one with $\tau_{mc} = 1$, and, as usual, when there are two pure strategy equilibria there is also a mixed strategy equilibrium with $\tau_{mc} \in (0, 1)$.

This multiplicity arises only for some parameters; for others there is a unique steady state with $N_m > 0$, which is B^T if ρ_m is small, B^K if ρ_m is big, and B^R if ρ_m is in between. But at least for *some* nondegenerate set of parameters there is multiplicity. Why? There are two necessary ingredients: $\rho_m > 0$, and N_m endogenous.

Here is the intuition. Suppose $\tau_{mc} = 0$, which is like a buy-and-hold strategy by M. That makes N_0 low (in fact, it is 0 in steady state, although that changes if there is depreciation, $\delta_p > 0$). When N_0 is low it is hard for P to trade, so few agents choose to act as P. That makes it hard for M to get x and hence makes M reluctant to trade it away, so $\tau_{mc} = 0$ is a best response. Now, suppose $\tau_{mc} = 1$. Then N_0 is high, making it easier for P to trade, so more agents act as P. Then it is easier for M to get x and so $\tau_{mc} = 1$ is a best response. For some parameters both outcomes are possible.

This discussion and Figure 4 concern steady states, but when there are multiple steady states there can also be multiple dynamic equilibria. These equilibria can display fluctuations even when fundamentals are constant: They are driven purely by beliefs, as self-fulfilling prophecies. Moreover, one can describe the outcomes in terms of market liquidity, which is greater with higher τ_{mc} since that means more trade. Again, for this multiplicity to arise we need endogenous market composition, plus $\rho_m > 0$, since a buy-and-hold strategy is never a good idea when $\rho_m \leq 0$. This can be interpreted as saying that intermediated markets for assets, with $\rho_m > 0$, can be fragile or volatile, but not intermediated markets for goods, with $\rho_m < 0$.

Gu et al. (2026) change that result and interpretation. They show in a generalized environment that similar multiplicity and volatility can arise with $\rho_m < 0$. There are various differences between the papers. One is that instead of endogenizing market composition by having some agents choose to act as either M or P, Gu et al. (2026) fix the measure of each type but let type P participate in the market only if they pay a cost κ. This is more standard than having agents choose to act as P or M, at least in the sense that it is similar to labor models following Pissarides (2000), where firms choose whether to enter, rather than having agents choose whether to be a worker or a firm (which is not to say that models of occupational choice are uninteresting).

A bigger difference is that Gu et al. (2026) have match-specific heterogeneity in buyers' valuations: When a seller, M or P, meets C the pair draw

u at random. This is interesting for its own sake and delivers nice results. First, M's decision about trading with C is characterized by a reservation value, R, such that they trade when $u > R$ and not when $u < R$, analogous to a reservation wage strategy in job search. It is immediate that $R = V_1 - V_0$ since u must be enough to cover M's loss from giving up inventory. Moreover, this is nice because R, and hence the probability of trade between M and C, varies smoothly with parameter changes and over time.

This introduces a new reason for M and C to not trade: The match-specific u is too low. Of course, C wants to trade even at low u as long as y is low, but $u < R$ means y would have to be too low for M to agree (the point is that trade requires mutual agreement). This effect is absent in Nosal et al. (2019), where M's alternative to trading with C is to enjoy the flow ρ_m, which is never a good alternative when $\rho_m < 0$. To be sure, $\rho_m > 0$ discourages trade between M and C – the way unemployment insurance discourages acceptance in job search, say – but we do not need $\rho_m > 0$ to get M and C to pass on trade.

The enhanced version of the story is this: Suppose M agents adopt a high reservation value R, which is not a buy-and-hold strategy, but a buy-and-hold-out (for a higher u) strategy. Then N_1 is high and N_0 low, making it hard for P to trade so fewer P agents enter, replacing the effect described earlier, which is that fewer agents choose to act as P. Still, the outcome is similar: a low N_p, making it hard for M to get x and rationalizing high R. But if instead M chooses low R then N_1 will be low and N_0 high, making it easier for type P to trade, so more P enter the market, making it easier for M to get inventory and rationalizing low R.

Hence, in this environment, multiplicity due to beliefs does not require $\rho_m > 0$. Not only can there be multiple steady states here, there can be dynamic equilibria where trading strategies and market composition vary over time. Gu et al. (2026) use dynamical system theory to prove the existence of continuous time limit cycles – that is, equilibria where endogenous variables fluctuate in the long run – but since the methods are somewhat technical, using bifurcation theory, we do not go into detail (it is not that the math is especially difficult, with Azariadis 1993, e.g., providing a textbook treatment geared to economists, but we think in this Element our time and space are better spent on other issues).

However, it is worth noting that the methods used by Gu et al. (2026) are difficult (if not impossible) to apply in Nosal et al. (2019), where u is degenerate, because with u degenerate the dynamical system is not smooth: The probability that M trades with C jumps from 0 to 1 as the system goes from $V_1 - V_0 > u$ to $V_1 - V_0 < u$. Hence, the existence of equilibrium cycles is not verified in that paper; in Gu et al. (2026) it is verified.

5 Private Information

Middlemen are often regarded as experts in assessing product quality, giving them a prominent role in markets for used cars, precious stones, antiques, art, etcetera. These markets are plagued by asymmetric information in the sense of Akerlof (1970). Do information frictions explain the emergence of middlemen? Do expert middlemen improve welfare? To address these questions, some papers incorporate information frictions into a middlemen framework.[17] In this section we introduce two of them.

Li (1998) is similar in spirit to the Rubinstein–Wolinsky framework, while Biglaiser and Li (2018) model a one-shot game emphasizing adverse selection. In both cases, product quality is an endogenous decision of producers, and with information frictions their decision depends on others' beliefs, which must be consistent with equilibrium. This self-fulfilling feature naturally supports multiple equilibria. Li (1998) highlights this kind of multiplicity, while Biglaiser and Li (2018) focus on cases with a unique equilibrium.

Li's (1998) model is related to Williamson and Wright (1994), which is simplistic in the sense that all goods are indivisible, but such models can still make interesting points. Time is continuous and there are random bilateral meetings. A continuum of homogenous agents produce, trade, and consume a good which can be of low or high quality, $j \in \{L, H\}$. The L good costs 0 and yields 0 utility from consumption; the H good costs $c > 0$ and yields utility $u > c$. All agents have the option of becoming M by paying a fixed cost κ that can be interpreted as acquiring a quality-testing technology, in addition to c, the cost to produce an H good. Let A denote traders that do not choose to act as middleman and normalize $N_a + N_m = 1$.

Assume A can verify whether quality is L or H with probability $\sigma < 1$, while M can always verify quality. Agents first choose occupation, $i \in \{A, M\}$, then A agents choose $j \in \{L, H\}$. When agents meet they decide whether to trade after potentially verifying quality, and note that the occupation, M or A, is recognizable upon meeting. When two As trade, they simply swap goods.

[17] Other papers modeling middlemen being good at verifying quality include Biglaiser (1993), Biglaiser and Friedman (1994), and Biglaiser and Friedman (1999). Several others focus on different information structures. Garella (1989) shows that middlemen can randomize offers to address adverse selection. In Gehrig (1993), buyers and sellers differ in valuations and costs that are private information, which can lead them to trade via intermediaries. Lizzeri (1999) and Albano and Lizzeri (2001) study information revelation by certification intermediaries. Kariv et al. (2018) model middlemen's financial capacities as private information. Lester et al. (2023) consider dealers who learn asset quality over time in an OTC market. Jovanovic and Menkveld (2024) analyze middlemen with superior information about the common value of an asset. As is perhaps unsurprising, private information models depend a lot on modeling details.

When A trades with M, assume that M makes a take-it-or-leave-it offer: M gives up $1 - y_j$ units of the good for A's whole unit, and A consumes what they receive, while M consumes y_j and seeks to retrade the good.[18] Upon consuming once, A starts over by again choosing i, as does M after completing one round of intermediation (as discussed earlier in the context of other models, here everyone is in the market forever).

Note that M may have an incentive to accept L goods, as they get to consume $1 + y_j$ units of H goods from each round of intermediation. Thus, there are in principle four types, $ij \in \{ah, a\ell, mh, m\ell\}$, capturing occupation and inventory, and V_{ij} indicates the corresponding payoffs. In equilibrium, the best response for occupational choice satisfies

$$N_m = \begin{cases} 1 & \text{if } V_{ah} < V_{mh} - \kappa \\ [0,1] & \text{if } V_{ah} = V_{mh} - \kappa \\ 0 & \text{if } V_{ah} > V_{mh} - \kappa. \end{cases} \tag{32}$$

The participation condition for M with L good is $V_{m\ell} \geq 0$. The production decision satisfies

$$N_{ah} = \begin{cases} N_a & \text{if } V_{ah} - c > V_{a\ell} \\ [0, N_a] & \text{if } V_{ah} - c = V_{a\ell} \\ 0 & \text{if } V_{ah} - c < V_{a\ell}. \end{cases} \tag{33}$$

Two other best responses are whether A accepts unknown quality and whether M accepts L. If M never accepts L, they are honest; if M always accepts L, they are dishonest; and they may mix in between. These decisions depend on others' beliefs and strategies. In equilibrium, individual strategies must be consistent with beliefs.

This model captures the following aspects of middlemen: they emerge endogenously; they have an informational advantage over others; and they may or may not be trustworthy. It is shown that when σ and κ are low, there are active M and they always trade high-quality goods. This means M choose to be honest because there are enough informed agents playing a disciplinary role. For moderately high σ, M can mix, trading both L and H goods. When σ is even higher, there are multiple equilibria, with $N_m = 0$ and $N_{ah} = N_a$ as well as with $N_m > 0$ and $N_{ah} < N_a$. See Figure 5.

In this framework, M improves efficiency by increasing A's incentives to produce high quality, and consequently improving A's acceptance of high

[18] Note that A has the outside option – wait for another A – so they get a positive payoff even with take-it-or-leave-it offers by M.

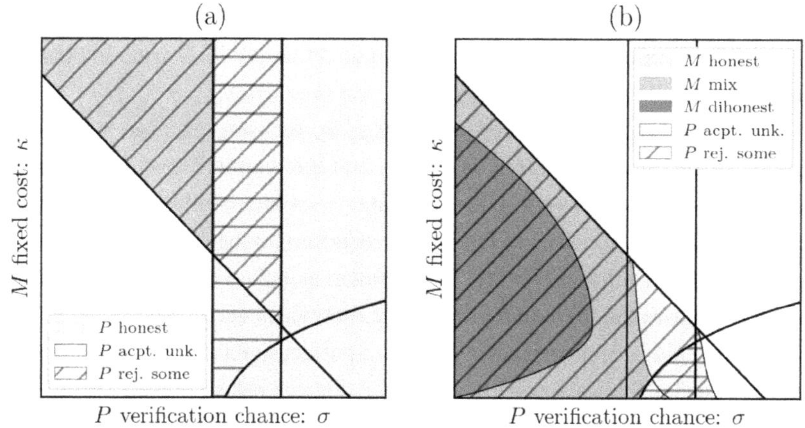

Figure 5 Equilibrium set with (panel (b)) and without (panel (a)) middlemen.

quality. However, M spends more time trading rather than producing, so higher N_m reduces total output. These two forces determine M's impact on welfare. Though across equilibria with $N_m = 0$ and $N_m > 0$, M can be welfare improving, the occupational choice is typically suboptimal. Specifically, Li (1998) shows N_m is too big.

The approach in Biglaiser and Li (2018) is different: Agents have fixed types – P, M and C – and the paper compares equilibrium outcomes with and without M. In their baseline model, P pays $c(e)$ for effort e that affects the probability of producing H goods. Again, H good yields u for C and L good yields 0. Here M do not get utility from consuming the good, but profit from payments in the form of transferable utility. Also, M faces an entry cost κ to be active.

In terms of quality verification, M's technology is no longer perfect: They receive a noisy signal that is correct with probability σ_m, which still gives M an advantage over other agents who receive an inferior signal, which is correct with probability $\sigma_c < \sigma_m$. The imperfect signal induces a misidentification effect, where P with L generates a positive signal with M. The opportunity to fool M gives P an additional avenue besides selling directly to buyers L goods pretending to be H goods, which always reduces P's incentive to invest in quality. This means the presence of M can reduce welfare via this effect.

Meanwhile, instead of meeting each other randomly, the agents here meet sequentially. Consider $N_p = N_m = 1$ and $N_c = 2$. After producing a unit, P first meets M, who receives a private signal and makes a take-it-or-leave-it offer. If P and M trade, M brings the good to C; if P and M do not trade, P seeks to trade with C. Then both Cs receive a public signal and bid independently and simultaneously, with the winner getting the good. This sequential structure induces adverse selection: As M is more likely to trade with H, C rationally adjust their belief about P's quality in direct trades. This again lowers the incentive for P to invest in quality.

Biglaiser and Li (2018) show uniqueness by focusing on cases where the cost κ of becoming type M is moderate, and the marginal cost c' of quality is either high or low (but not intermediate, since intermediate marginal cost might induce multiplicity). In this case, in equilibrium, better information does not necessarily improve welfare. In particular, as $\sigma_m \to 1$, it turns out that P always chooses the minimum effort. Note that whenever C encounters P, the latter has already been rejected by M with a perfect signal. Therefore, C agents believe such a P always carries L goods and hence refuse to trade. It follows that when P trades with M, P loses the outside option of trading with C. Given that M makes a take-it-or-leave offer, P faces a severe holdup problem and thus never exerts effort.

Not only can better technology reduce welfare, greater competition can as well. Intuitively, when many M obtain private signals and compete, a P who shows up in direct trade must be holding L goods, which again eliminates P's outside option of trading with C and induces minimum effort. This result follows from the sequential structure of the model. Spulber (2002) also studies intermediated trade with asymmetric information, but in his setup P, M, and C move simultaneously, and then competition among M agents improves welfare.

From these papers one sees that information and intermediation can interact in complex ways. While M may be active due to information frictions, the welfare effects are ambiguous. A better verification technology undoubtedly reduces informational asymmetries, but the resulting impact on occupational choice and adverse selection can offset or even reverse the benefits of better information. Such results are important and suggest that even more work should be done on intermediation and information.

6 Intermediation Chains and Bubbles

Wright and Wong (2014) study middlemen chains, asking how they form, how many intermediaries might be in a chain, and how bargaining at one link in the chain depends on bargaining at future links. This is relevant since in reality there are often multiple middlemen engaged in getting goods (or inputs or assets) from originators to end users: for example, from farmer to broker to distributor to retailer to consumer.

Internet trade provides a prominent example of these structures. Many advertised wholesalers are actually intermediaries operating within a chain

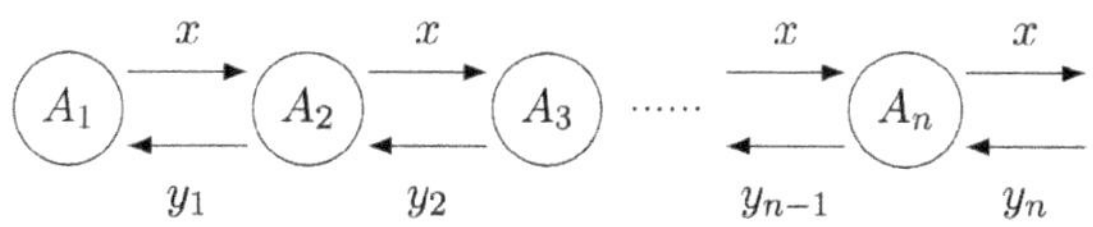

Figure 6 Market structure consistent with Wright–Wong (2014).

of middlemen. This occurs when a business purchases products from a wholesale company that has itself sourced them from another wholesaler, potentially continuing through multiple layers.

Another example concerns real estate flipping, where a property is purchased and quickly resold for profit. Under a multiple investor flip, one investor acquires a property below market value and sells it to a second investor, who then sells it to the final consumer at a price closer to market value. These profits are typically generated by buying low and selling high in a rising market or by renovating a property before resale.

Here agents acting as middlemen do not have an advantage in information or technology, they are simply a necessary part of the process of getting goods from suppliers to end users. An interpretation (suggested by Dale Mortensen; see fn. 18) is that to move goods from location A_1 to A_N, they must travel through $A_2, A_3 \ldots$ and those with property rights to the intermediate locations all want a cut of the profits.[19] Figure 6 depicts the market structure – a simple network – and hence the potential transactions.

The formalization has time continuous and potentially unbounded, with a set of agents $\mathcal{A} = \{A_1, A_2, \ldots, A_N\}$, where N may or may not be finite. These agents are spatially separated: A_n can trade with A_{n-1} and A_{n+1} but no one else. Hence, trade between A_{n-1} and A_{n+1} must go through A_n, and there is no scope for cutting out the middleman.[20] The friction is that it takes time for A_n to meet A_{n+1}, with α_n the Poisson arrival rate. As noted earlier, there is an indivisible object x and a divisible object y, and A_1 is endowed with x. If A_n acquires x from A_{n-1}, then A_n can consume it for payoff u_n or try to trade it to A_{n+1} for y_n, which in general yields payoff $U_n(y_n)$. As discussed earlier,

[19] Mortensen's leading example is that to get wheat from northern to southern Europe, historically, one has to ship it though Ghent, which is interesting because he made the suggestion at the SED meetings in Ghent.

[20] It might be interesting to pursue an extension of this environment, where is it possible for A_{n-1} and A_{n+1} to cut out the middleman A_n, at some cost. On disintermediation, in general, practitioners ask: "why doesn't every wholesaler just buy from the manufacture and get the deepest discount? The answer is simple – not all wholesalers (or companies claiming to be wholesalers) can afford to purchase the minimum bulk-order requirements that a manufacture requires. Secondly, many manufactures only do business with companies that are established" (Ellis 2009). More theoretical work on this would be welcome.

$U_n(y_n) = y_n$ corresponds to transferable utility, but it is also interesting to consider $U''(y) < 0$ later in this section.

The Wright and Wong (2014) model uses a particular bargaining protocol that is nice but not crucial for the results – all that really matters is that agents trade when there are gains from trade. In any case, if A_n with x does not consume x, but tries to trade it, the flow payoff is $rV_n = \alpha_n [U_n(y_n) - V_n] - c_n$, or

$$V_n = \frac{\alpha_n U_n(y_n) - c_n}{r + \alpha_n}, \tag{34}$$

where c_n is an n-specific search or storage cost. Then A_n wants to trade when $V_n \geq u_n$. If $N < \infty$ equilibrium is found by starting at the last link in the chain, where A_{N-1} with x meets A_N, since N must consume x – there is no one left with whom to trade. Hence, $u_N < u_{N-1}$ implies A_{N-1} consumes x and $u_N > u_{N-1}$ implies A_N consumes it after giving y_{N-1} to A_{N-1}. Assuming $U(y) = y$, we get

$$V_{N-1} = \frac{\alpha_{N-1}[\theta_{N-1}u_N + (1-\theta_{N-1})u_{N-1}] - c_{N-1}}{r + \alpha_{N-1}}, \tag{35}$$

after inserting y_{N-1}, where θ_n is bargaining power. Hence, search by A_{N-1} requires $u_{N-1} \leq V_{N-1}$, or

$$u_{N-1} \leq \frac{\alpha_{N-1}\theta_{N-1}u_N - c_{N-1}}{r + \alpha_{N-1}\theta_{N-1}} \equiv u^*_{N-1}. \tag{36}$$

If $N < \infty$ there is generically a unique equilibrium that, depending on parameters, can involve anything from A_1 consuming x to the opposite extreme, where A_N consumes it. In general, there is maximal length of the intermediation chain. If the environment is stationary (parameters are the same for all n) then one can check that as times moves forward, so that x is getting closer to its end user, y_{N-n} increases with every trade, and, in fact, it increases at an increasing rate.[21]

To expand on the results, let T_n be the random date when A_n trades x to A_{n+1}. Since the arrival times are Poisson, the interarrival times $T_n - T_{n-1}$ are distributed exponentially (see any source on stochastic processes, e.g., Çinlar (1975)). This means there is a high probability of short interarrival times and a low probability of long interarrival times, and so typical realizations have trades *clustered*, with many exchanges occurring in relatively rapid succession, separated by long periods of inactivity. This might look like

[21] Li and Schurhoff (2019) document the empirical distributions of intermediation chain lengths and intermediation markups in municipal bonds. Hugonnier et al. (2020) further calibrate a model with richer heterogeneity to match these distributions.

bubbles in the market, with long lulls interspersed by trading frenzies where y_n accelerates over time. But y_n accelerates only because x is getting closer and closer to the end user, and Poisson arrivals are memoryless, so there are no bubbles, or frenzies and lulls, in any meaningful economic sense.[22]

However, there can be genuine bubbles when $N = \infty$, related to standard results in monetary theory. To pursue this, first note that money and middlemen papers would take diametric positions on this: The former would say y is a good and x is money; the latter would say the opposite. Which makes more sense? Well, y being divisible is a point in favor of middlemen papers, since divisibility is a property commonly associated with money, but we think that should not be given much weight compared to the functional definition of money: that it is a store of value and medium of exchange.

Clearly, it is x and not y that is a store of value: x is a durable object that when acquired lets A_n enjoy a payoff at some future date. And it is a medium of exchange according to standard usage – an object accepted in trade not to be consumed or used in production but to be traded again later. Indeed, x solves the standard double-coincidence problem that makes money useful: When A_n wants y from A_{n+1}, the only way to pay is by transferring x. On these grounds, x looks like money.

Does this matter for anything? Maybe. It determines who should be called buyers and sellers and what defines the price. In nonmonetary exchange – A gives B apples for bananas – it is not meaningful to call either a buyer or a seller. But if A gives B apples in exchange for cash then A is the seller and B is the buyer. While one can use words as one likes, would anyone suggest, for example, reversing the worker and firm labels in standard labor-market models? One could prove similar results, but it matters for substantive questions – for example, should we tax/subsidize workers or firms? It similarly makes a difference for who we call buyers and sellers – for example, should we tax/subsidize shoppers or retailers? Moreover, normalizing the size of x to 1, if y is money and x is a good the price is y, while if y is a good and x is money the price is $1/y$. This matters for the foregoing discussion of y accelerating – is that a hyper-inflation or a hyper-deflation?

[22] As Çinlar (1975, pp. 79–80) says, "this [exponential density of interarrival times] is monotone decreasing. As a result, an interarrival time is more likely to have a length in $[0, s]$ than in a length in $[t, t + s]$ for any t. Thus, a Poisson process has more short intervals than long ones. Therefore, a plot of the time series of arrivals on a line looks, to the naive eye, as if the arrivals occur in clusters." Yet Poisson processes are memoryless: "Knowing that an interarrival time has already lasted t units does not alter the probability of its lasting another s units." This is all standard, but perhaps underappreciated in economics.

So, one can think of x as a good potentially passing from originator to end user via a chain of intermediaries trading at each link for y_n; or, one can think of x as a medium of exchange allowing agents to acquire y. This is one reason to allow nonlinear $U(y)$. There is another reason. Suppose $N = \infty$. As is understood in monetary economics, there can be bubbles in the sense that no one ever consumes x, agents just keep trading it, like a vintage wine market where people trade and retrade bottles no one will ever drink, or a POW camp where prisoners trade cigarettes no one will ever smoke. Moreover, y can be above the fundamental value of x, given by the utility of consuming it. There exist such bubbly equilibria here if $U''(y) < 0$, but not if $U(y)$ is linear (see Wright and Wong 2014 for details).

We pursue something similar but more sophisticated: the application in Awaya et al. (2022). That paper constructs a finite-period model of bubbles where the indivisible good is considered an asset. In contrast to the specification given earlier, where bubbles can occur only if there are an infinite number of middlemen and periods, Awaya et al. demonstrate that bubbles can occur with a finite number of traders and periods. When the horizon is finite, a standard backward induction argument implies that, if everything is common knowledge, bubbles never occur. Awaya et al. relax the assumption of common knowledge and consider higher-order uncertainty. This means that even if every agent knows the fundamental value of the asset is 0, agents may not know whether other agents know it.

The information structure is key here. Following the definition of strong bubbles in Allen et al. (1993), a bubble occurs if all agents know the indivisible asset is worthless but it is traded for a positive amount of the divisible good. There are two necessary ingredients for this. First, there must be at least one agent who may not know the consumption value of the asset for A_N – otherwise, the value is commonly known and the asset can never be overpriced. Second, there must be some situations where the consumption value of the asset for A_N is zero and all agents know it.

To capture this, assume that all parameters describing utilities, costs, etcetera, are common knowledge, except for the consumption value of the asset for A_N. Awaya et al. assume that, prior to trade, all agents except A_N observe the consumption value of the asset for A_N. Hence, the initial owner and the middlemen are experts who always know the value of the asset, while the final user is not an expert and may not know.[23]

[23] Glode and Opp (2016) study intermediation chains under a different information structure, in which later users possess more information than earlier ones. Their focus is not on bubbles, but on the welfare implications of adding partially informed middlemen.

If the consumption value of the asset for the end user A_N is 0, then A_N receives a signal with some probability; otherwise, A_N does not receive a signal. Thus, if A_N receives a signal, A_N is sure that the consumption value of the asset for A_N is 0, and every other agent also knows the asset is worthless. Moreover, if A_N receives a signal, A_N (nonstrategically) sends a signal to A_{N-1}. The signal reaches A_{N-1} with some probability but can also be lost. Thus, if A_{N-1} receives a signal, A_{N-1} is sure that A_N knows that the consumption value for A_N is 0. Similarly, if A_{N-1} receives a signal from A_N, then A_{N-1} (nonstrategically) sends a signal to A_{N-2}. Again, the signal reaches A_{N-2} with some probability but could be lost. This process continues until a signal is lost between some two agents or the initial owner A_1 receives a signal. In words, the signal (rumor) that A_N knows that the asset is worthless spreads from A_N to A_1, but it is subject to loss between any two agents.

With this information structure, bubbles occur at some states. Consider the state where the consumption value of the asset for the final user A_N is 0 and the signal between A_{n^*} and A_{n^*-1} is lost for some $n^* \geq 3$. In this state, $A_N, \ldots, A_{n^*}$ receive signals, while the rest do not. Given this realization, since A_N receives a signal, every agent knows that the asset is worthless. Yet the asset is exchanged for $n^* - 2$ periods, until it reaches A_{n^*-1}. This is a bubble. If it were common knowledge that the consumption value of the asset for A_N is 0, the asset would not trade. Therefore, higher-order uncertainty is necessary for bubbles. At period $n^* - 1$, agent A_{n^*} refuses to trade with A_{n^*-1} and the bubble bursts. This is because A_{n^*} knows that A_{n^*+1} knows that... that A_N knows that the consumption value of the asset for A_N is 0, and hence, A_{n^*} knows that A_{n^*} cannot sell the asset to A_{n^*+1}.

Middlemen here are necessary for bubbles. Without them, there is just the initial owner and the final user, and if both know the asset is worthless they do not trade and bubbles do not occur. In this sense, middlemen are a source of instability. Awaya et al. (2022) also characterize prices during bubbles, interpreting the asset price as y_t. This price is not only increasing, it is accelerating during bubbles, because middlemen must be compensated for the risk that they may not be able to retrade the asset. That is, this price accelerates because the probability that a middleman can sell it decreases over time, so those who trade in later periods are exposed to more risk, and the price compensates for that.

In a follow-up paper, Awaya et al. (2025)[24] integrate their analysis of bubbles into the monetary model of Lagos and Wright (2005) to study, among other

[24] Awaya, Y., Iwasaki, K., and Watanabe, M. (2025) "Money is the root of asset bubbles," unpublished working paper.

things, how a monetary policy affects the results. They show that the existence of bubbles depends on the degree of money injection. This is frontier research and a nice example of what one can do in models that incorporate both money and middlemen, which is discussed further in Section 9. Before going there, however, it is a good time to discuss work that amends some of the basic assumptions in the benchmark model.

7 Inventories and Directed Search

The models presented so far focus on $I \in \{0, 1\}$. In reality, inventory and variety are common attributes of retailers and dealers. A few papers go beyond this restriction. Nosal et al. (2019) have an extension of their baseline model with $I \in \{0, 1, \ldots, \hat{I}\}$ that they study using numerical methods, but we will not go into that. Instead, we highlight two other strands in the literature: One examines the distribution of middlemen's inventory size and composition with random search; the other focuses on the impact of inventory with directed search. Note that the inventories in this section take discrete values, which has implications for matching.[25]

Shevchenko (2004) relaxes the assumption of fixed inventory size in an environment with a continuum of agents and K different goods.[26] Agents have heterogeneous tastes for goods: agent i produces good i at 0 cost (for simplicity) and desires another good drawn at random. Since they both consume and produce, we do not label them as C or P and simply call these agents type A. They can trade bilaterally when they meet if there is a double coincidence of wants, where each one likes the good the other produces. In addition, A can meet M, a middleman. Type M have a cost to enter the market, so the measure N_m is endogenous. Also, each M maintains a capacity $\hat{I}$ – the number of shelves – by paying a flow cost $c(\hat{I})$, allowing them to store $\hat{I}$ goods. The cost of getting the initial inventory $\hat{I}$ is part of M's cost of entering the market.

In steady state, if A and M meet and M has in stock the variety that A wants, trade occurs. The way it works is this: A gives the good that A produces to M, who puts it on the shelf that opens up by taking the good A likes off the shelf; then A consumes some fraction θ of the good while M consumes the rest.

25 This contrasts with some other papers that study divisible inventories; that does not affect the matching process, but adds an intensive margin of trade (Lagos and Rocheteau 2009; Üslü 2019; Gong and Wright 2024; Gong et al. 2025).

26 Another paper considering inventory/capacity is Johri and Leach (2002), which allows $I \in \{0, 1, 2\}$ and emphasizes the distribution of heterogenous tastes. One more is Smith (2004), featuring a location model where M choose capacity and C search sequentially.

This can be interpreted as M having a technology to transform any good into something M likes, with the cost of the technology being part of their operating cost $c(\hat{I})$.

Shevchenko (2004) demonstrates the existence of a unique and stable steady-state distribution of inventories – all M have the same shelf size $\hat{I}$ and the variety distribution is uniform across M. He shows that size $\hat{I}$ increases with M's bargaining power and arrival rate. In terms of welfare, on the intensive margin, middlemen always understock relative to the optimum: $\hat{I}$ is too small. This occurs because M chooses $\hat{I}$ upon entering the market, and the cost $c(\hat{I})$ is sunk when A shows up. The resulting hold-up problem makes $\hat{I}$ too low. On the extensive margin, the number of M can be too big or too small, depending on parameter values.

In the aforementioned formulation M's choice of $\hat{I}$ does not affect their arrival rate: meetings are purely random. Now consider a situation where buyers can choose where to search – which shop to visit – based on the size of their inventory. This suggests a directed search approach, where consumers select sellers based on their posted prices plus their inventory, which is assumed to be observable. Directed search provides an interesting and (in some contexts) realistic way to endogenize trading patterns.

Watanabe (2010) describes a static game in which middlemen can have multiple units in inventory and can transact with multiple agents simultaneously. Because they can serve multiple agents, the matching process is many-to-one. Watanabe adopts a coordination game framework, as in Burdett et al. (2001). If a seller has $\hat{I}$ units of the good, and more than $\hat{I}$ buyers show up, only $\hat{I}$ of them get the good. This endogenously generates the number of trades as an urn-ball technology.

With a continuum of agents, the equilibrium can be characterized by best responses and the market utility condition that all sellers must provide the same expected payoff to buyers. Intuitively, if one seller offers a higher expected payoff, buyers will have an incentive to go to that seller, pushing the equilibrium toward payoff equivalence. The implication is that, by holding more inventory, middlemen reduce their probability of stockouts, and hence can charge more than producers who can serve at most one customer. The ability to have multiple units in inventory thus gives M a role.

Watanabe establishes an equilibrium in which a unit mass of agents choose to be acting as type P or M, and the latter obtain inventories from P in a competitive wholesale market. With a fixed cost κ to become a middleman, N_m is determined by $V_m - V_p = \kappa$. Occupational diversity here requires indifference if agents are ex ante homogenous. If agents are heterogenous, occupational choice typically leads to cutoff rules, similar to, for example, the models in Masters (2007, 2008).

When $N_c > N_p + N_m$, there is a unique equilibrium with intermediated trade, $N_m > 0$. In contrast, when $N_c < N_p + N_m$, an equilibrium with $N_m > 0$ requires a low $\hat{I}$, and multiple equilibria can arise: one with high N_m, high p_m, and small $\hat{I}$, and another with low N_m, low p_m, and large $\hat{I}$. Multiplicity here stems from the nonmonotone nature of the spread $p_{mc} - p_{pm}$ in capacity $\hat{I}$. This is supported by empirical evidence (e.g., Dana and Spier 2001 on video rentals; Li et al. 2024 on used cars; Aguirregabiria 1999 on supermarkets; Leslie 2004 on theater tickets). Watanabe (2010) also shows that the equilibrium with many small middlemen is stable but inefficient, whereas the one with fewer large middlemen is unstable but more efficient.

Recall that in Shevchenko (2004) inventory and variety play a role, whereas Watanabe (2010, 2020) considers inventory but not variety. Moraga-Gonzalez and Watanabe (2023) incorporate variety into a directed search environment while maintaining capacity $\hat{I}$. Specifically, goods are differentiated, and consumers learn their match-specific value upon visiting a seller. The matching function is accordingly generalized: When $\hat{I} = 1$, it follows an urn-ball specification; as $\hat{I} \to \infty$, it converges to a weighted urn-ball technology (see, e.g., Lester et al. 2017), with the weights reflecting match-specific values. The equilibrium price is inefficiently high, except in the limit as $\hat{I} \to \infty$. In addition to variety, Rhodes et al. (2021) incorporate cross-product externalities and show how variety alone can justify the emergence of middlemen.

In sum, inventory size and variety are potential sources of M's advantage, distinct from capabilities like bargaining power or search efficiency. When their advantage comes from bargaining or search, one can determine whether replacing P with M generates surplus. Inventory and variety, by contrast, create a middlemen advantage through the matching process and the implied terms of trade.

In addition to providing some microfoundations for M's higher meeting probabilities, directed search provides an alternative way to endogenize prices, capturing the role of middlemen in posting publicly observable terms of trade (Spulber 1996b). This insight is sharpened by Watanabe (2018), who contrasts random search and bargaining, on the one hand, with directed search and posting, on the other hand. While the existing models and results are nice, this is a branch of the literature that merits even more research.[27]

[27] Geromichalos (2012, 2014) also models multi-unit trading with directed search, though he does not focus on middlemen.

8 Intermediation in Finance

Many financial markets are highly intermediated. In OTC asset markets, investors who want to trade must search for counterparties and negotiate the terms of trade. Duffie et al. (2005) provide a model of OTC trade that sheds light on many issues, including standard measures of liquidity, like bid-ask spreads, execution delays, and trading volume.[28] These models share some features with those discussed elsewhere in this Element, but differ in other aspects.

In the typical finance paper, there are no producers or consumers – the object being traded, denoted x as usual, is an indivisible asset in fixed supply X. A fixed set of agents, labeled A, get a flow return ρ from holding the asset, and as in many other models individual inventories are restricted to $i \in \{0, 1\}$. Assuming X is scarce (i.e., there are fewer assets than agents), gains from trade are generated by random idiosyncratic valuations. Namely, these agents have a state variable given by ρ_h or $\rho_\ell < \rho_h$, and according to Poison process this valuation switches over time from ρ_j to $\rho_{j'}$ at rate $\omega_{jj'}$, independent of i.

So at any point in time there can be some agents with low valuation ρ_ℓ and $i = 1$, as well as some with high valuation ρ_h and $i = 0$. If they meet there are gains from trade, with payments made in transferable utility, which again we interpret in terms of another good anyone can produce with constant marginal cost and anyone can consume with constant marginal utility. Let V_{ij} be A's value function with asset position i and valuation j and let $\Delta_j \equiv V_{1j} - V_{0j}$. It is immediate that A trades with another A when one has $ij = 1\ell$ while the other has $ij = 0h$.

In addition to type A agents, there are type M agents, often called dealers in these papers, who can buy and sell assets. For simplicity, suppose they get 0 return from holding the asset, but, in fact, usually in these models M never holds inventory, with exceptions like Weill (2007, 2008) or Gavazza (2011). The reason is that they can always access a competitive, frictionless interdealer market (with type A excluded from this market). Therefore, M in contact with A that has ρ_ℓ and $i = 1$ can in principle buy the asset from A and sell it on the

[28] This search-and-bargaining framework is complementary to other approaches in finance. One virtue is its realism: "Many assets, such as mortgage-backed securities, corporate bonds, government bonds, US federal funds, emerging-market debt, bank loans, swaps and many other derivatives, private equity, and real estate, are traded in . . . [over-the-counter] markets. Traders in these markets search for counterparties, incurring opportunity or other costs. When counterparties meet, their bilateral relationship is strategic; prices are set through a bargaining process that reflects each investor's alternatives to immediate trade" (Duffie et al. 2007, p. 1865).

interdealer market, while M in contact with A that has ρ_h and $i = 0$ can sell the asset to A while acquiring it on the interdealer market.[29]

In the interdealer market, it is not generally the case that the number of type A trying to buy the indivisible asset from M equals the number of type A trying to sell it to M. Hence, the interdealer price makes M and A on the long side of the market indifferent to trade, with the number of such trades set to get what is needed on the short side: If $N_{1\ell} < N_{0h}$, then M meet more potential buyers than sellers and the interdealer price is $y_m = y_{1m} = \Delta_h$; and if $N_{1\ell} > N_{0h}$, then $y_m = y_{m0} = \Delta_\ell$.

As usual, what is called the bid price y_{m0} and ask price y_{1m} are determined through bargaining, with θ_m being M's share of the surplus, which is $S_{1m} = \Delta_h - y_m$ or $S_{m0} = y_m - \Delta_\ell$ when selling or buying. It follows that

$$y_{m0} = \theta_m \Delta_h + (1 - \theta_m) y_m, \tag{37}$$

$$y_{1m} = \theta_m \Delta_\ell + (1 - \theta_m) y_m. \tag{38}$$

The bid-ask spread $y_{m0} - y_{1m}$ is a common indicator of asset market friction. The price y_a between two agents of type A is also determined by bargaining, with θ_a being the surplus share of the one bringing the asset to the meeting.

Normalize the measure of A with $\sum_{i,j} N_{ij} = 1$, where N_{ij} is the proportion of A with position i and valuation j. Denote by α_m and α_a the Poisson rates of A meeting M and A meeting A. The dynamic programming equations are

$$rV_{1h} = \omega_{h\ell} (V_{1\ell} - V_{1h}) + \rho_h + \dot{V}_{1h}, \tag{39}$$

$$rV_{0h} = \omega_{h\ell} (V_{0\ell} - V_{0h}) + \alpha_a N_{1\ell} (\Delta_h - y_a) + \alpha_m (\Delta_h - y_{m0}) + \dot{V}_{0h}, \tag{40}$$

$$\begin{aligned} rV_{1\ell} = {} & \omega_{\ell h} (V_{1h} - V_{1\ell}) + \alpha_a N_{0h} (y_a - \Delta_\ell) \\ & + \alpha_m (y_{1m} - \Delta_\ell) + \rho_\ell + \dot{V}_{1\ell}, \end{aligned} \tag{41}$$

$$rV_{0\ell} = \omega_{\ell h} (V_{0h} - V_{0\ell}) + \dot{V}_{0\ell}. \tag{42}$$

In words, (41) says the flow value $rV_{1\ell}$ is: the rate $\omega_{\ell h}$ at which ρ switches from ℓ to h times the change $V_{1h} - V_{1\ell}$; plus the rate α_a at which A meets another A, times the probability the other one wants to trade N_{0h}, times 1ℓ's surplus; plus the rate α_m at which A meets M times the surplus for A trading with M; plus the pure rate of change over time $\dot{V}_{1\ell}$. The others are similar.

[29] One can dispense with the frictionless interdealer market by assuming there are intermediary firms with many individual middlemen, akin to the large families in Shi (1997); this allows them to balance buying and selling activity within the firm instead of in the interdealer market (see Trejos and Wright 2016). Both devices – Walrasian interdealer markets and many-dealer firms – are technical devices that can be more or less useful and reasonable depending on the application.

The laws of motion satisfy

$$\dot{N}_{1h} = N_{1\ell}\omega_{\ell h} - N_{1h}\omega_{h\ell} + N_{0h}\left(\alpha_a N_{1\ell} + \alpha_m\right), \tag{43}$$

$$\dot{N}_{0h} = N_{0\ell}\omega_{\ell h} - N_{0h}\omega_{h\ell} - N_{0h}\left(\alpha_a N_{1\ell} + \alpha_m\right), \tag{44}$$

$$\dot{N}_{1\ell} = N_{1h}\omega_{h\ell} - N_{1\ell}\omega_{\ell h} - N_{1\ell}\left(\alpha_a N_{0h} + \alpha_m\right), \tag{45}$$

$$\dot{N}_{0\ell} = N_{0h}\omega_{h\ell} - N_{0\ell}\omega_{\ell h} + N_{1\ell}\left(\alpha_a N_{0h} + \alpha_m\right). \tag{46}$$

An equilibrium is a list $(\mathbf{V}, \tau, \mathbf{N})$ satisfying the usual conditions, and it exists uniquely (Trejos and Wright 2016). From this, the terms of trade, the bid-ask spread, and other endogenous variables are easily recovered.

This stylized structure, with a core of dealers and a periphery of others that may trade directly or with dealers, is a reasonable representation of many OTC markets. The proportion of intermediated trade is $\alpha_m/(\alpha_m + \alpha_a N_{1\ell})$. Hence, the majority of exchanges can be direct, or intermediated, depending on parameters. A simple case where $\alpha_a = 0$ is nice since it makes the Vs and ys independent of N_{ij}. That makes it easy to see that spreads are decreasing in α_m and increasing in θ_m. Also, as $r \to 0$, y_{1m}, y_{m0}, and y_m all go to the same limit, which is ρ_ℓ/r if $X > \omega_{h\ell}/(\omega_{\ell h} + \omega_{h\ell})$ and ρ_h/r if $X < \omega_{h\ell}/(\omega_{\ell h} + \omega_{h\ell})$.

There are also implications for trade volume, often associated with liquidity, but these are sensitive to $i \in \{0,1\}$. That inventory restriction is relaxed in Lagos and Rocheteau (2009) and Üslü (2019), who have continuous asset positions. Another extension is Farboodi et al. (2025), who stick to $i \in \{0,1\}$, but their environment has no type M. Instead, intermediation emerges since agents differ in bargaining power.[30] Given transitory valuations as in Duffie et al. (2005), agents with stronger bargaining skills act as middlemen, buying assets from those with low bargaining power and low valuation, and selling to those with high valuation and low bargaining power.

This brings up a question: just because some agents buy now and sell later, are they middleman? If you bought a house in year the 2000 and sold it in 2025, perhaps because you were moving out of town, it does not seem reasonable to say that you were engaged in real estate intermediation (there are agents that are so engaged, and they are called real estate flippers). Type M in many of the models presented here are dedicated middlemen; agents in other models may

[30] There is a similar analysis in Farboodi et al. (2023), where agents differ in arrival rates. Although Masters (2007, 2008) focuses on goods, not assets, he similarly studies models where agents differ in production efficiency as well as bargaining power. His analysis is particularly insightful because it relies on comparative advantage: agents who act as middlemen are not necessarily good at intermediation, they are just bad at production (it's like the old adage: those who can, do; those who can't, teach).

trade a lot–say, because they have frequent preference shocks–but we are not convinced that they should be called intermediaries.

It may sound reasonable to think that a survey of middlemen in search equilibrium ought to provide a precise definition of a middleman, but doing so is not straightforward. The standard dictionary definition – "a person who buys goods from producers and sells them to retailers or consumers" – rings true, and is fully consistent with many of the models. Yet it is not immune to the housing example: you could have bought the property from a builder and sold it to someone who wants to live in it, or maybe flip it, and that does not make you a middleman. Perhaps a more holistic approach is better.

This ambiguity is not unique to the finance literature, as it applies, to a greater or lesser extent, in any of the models summarized here–although one could try to argue that it is more of an issue in settings where there is no producer or consumer of the object being traded. In any event, there are many papers building on the OTC framework, with or without dealers. Rather than discuss them in detail here, we refer readers to the recent and comprehensive book by Hugonnier et al. (2025).

However, we can discuss a connection between the finance literature and monetary economics. The OTC model with $\alpha_m = 0$ (no middlemen) is best for this comparison, even if in this Element that is not the most interesting case. In finance models following Duffie et al. (2005), gains from trade arise from heterogeneous valuations for x, with y serving as a payment instrument. Monetary models following Shi (1995) or Trejos and Wright (1995) have many of the same ingredients, but there are gains from trade in y and the asset x is used as a payment instrument. These gains from trade arise when $U(y) > C(y)$ for some y, which has quite a different implication than the transferable utility assumption with $U(y) = y = C(y)$. Trejos and Wright (2016) further explore the connection between the approaches, integrate them, and highlight some key results.[31] While this is not directly related to intermediation, it is good to understand the similarities and differences in the finance and monetary papers, especially since both purport to be about liquidity.

[31] Here is a quick summary: In the finance models equilibrium is unique, with transitional dynamics following from saddle-path stability; in the monetary model there are multiple stationary and nonstationary equilibria due to self-fulfilling prophecies. In the finance model with $\rho_\ell, \rho_h > 0$, there is trade if and only if an agent with ρ_ℓ and $i = 1$ meets one with ρ_h and $i = 0$; in the money model there is only one ρ, and hence no trade due to heterogeneous asset valuations, but given $U(y) - C(y) > 0$ for some y, there are gains from trading it. In the finance model, $\rho_\ell, \rho_h < 0$ implies agents stop trading and dispose of assets, while in money models the asset can be valued for its liquidity (i.e., as a means of payment) and hence traded even if $\rho < 0$ as long as $|\rho|$ is not too big. The integrated model, with gains from trading y plus heterogeneous ρs, inherits the above properties of the monetary models.

9 Money, Credit, and Middlemen

In general, money and middlemen provide a similar service: the institution of intermediated exchange and the institution of monetary exchange are both ways of ameliorating trading frictions. There are a few, but not very many, papers with both middlemen and money, even if it is recognized that there are connections between intermediation and payment economics.[32] Li (1999) is an early paper in this vein, showing how qualitative uncertainty over goods can give rise to both middlemen and fiat currency. In a pure barter economy, agents cannot verify the quality of goods they are offered, so some optimally invest in a costly inspection technology and thus become middlemen. These expert intermediaries can mitigate adverse-selection frictions while currency helps with double-coincidence frictions. This is a nice point, although the model in Li (1999) is simple, assuming indivisible goods and assets.

Urias (2018) has monetary trade in a model of middlemen that gets at some key ideas, but it is also somewhat restrictive in that producers are not allowed to trade directly with consumers. Gong (2018) uses a similar environment, but focuses on credit rather than money and lets producers try to trade directly with consumers, making equilibrium exchange pattern endogenous – it can have only direct trade in x from P to C, only indirect trade from P to M to C, or both, depending in a precise way on parameters. These papers build on the framework of Lagos and Wright (2005), which features sequential trade in different markets.

We can describe this in more detail following the presentation in Gong and Wright (2024). First, the model has something not in most middleman papers: To capture the intensive margin, x is divisible, which can be interpreted in terms of either quantity or quality. (To be precise, the extensive margin refers to the number of trades and the intensive margin refers to the size of trades.) While that is interesting in its own right, the bigger distinction from many previous models is the market structure, shown in Figure 7, interpretable as sequential trade in discrete time. First there is a wholesale market (WM) where P and M can, but C cannot, participate; then there is a retail market (RM) where C can trade with sellers, where these RM sellers can be either M that acquired x from P in WM, or P that did not trade with M in WM and try for direct trade in RM.

---

[32] As Spulber (1996a, p. 143) says, middlemen "hold inventories of goods on hand and stand ready to sell to customers. They further have cash on hand and stand ready to buy from suppliers. This avoids the problem of the coincidence of wants, in which a buyer and a seller need to want to transact with each other at the same time . . . In retail and wholesale markets, intermediaries provide similar immediacy services by standing ready to buy and sell commodities."

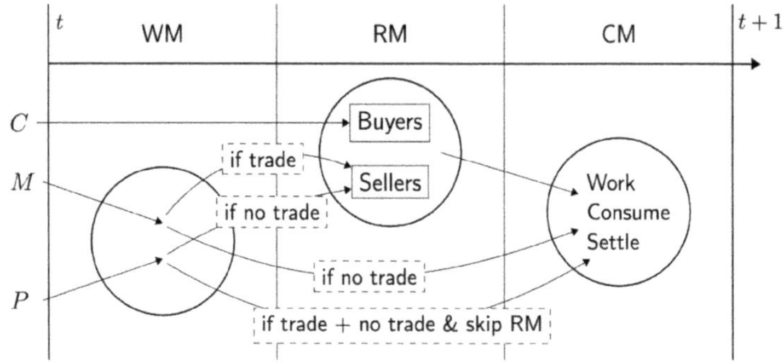

Figure 7 Market structure consistent with Gong (2018).

Sellers, both M and P, may or may not try to trade in RM because there is an entry cost κ.

After WM and RM, there convenes a frictionless centralized market (CM) where all agents work, consume, and adjust their assets or debt positions. In monetary versions, like Urias (2018), one's asset position can include currency; in credit versions, one's debt position can include accounts payable from purchases made in the previous WM or RM, plus accounts receivable from sales in the previous WM or RM. A common device in Lagos–Wright applications is to assume quasi-linear utility in consumption of a numeraire CM good (in fact, quasi-linearity can be relaxed, as in Wong 2016). Assuming interior solutions for CM optimization, this implies history independence: In money models, all agents of the same type leave the CM with the same cash; in credit models, all agents settle debts in the CM, and, moreover, one-period debt is without loss of generality.

This sequential structure replaces the three-sided market, where P, C, and M all participate, with two two-sided markets, one with P and M, and one with buyers and sellers, where buyers are type C while sellers can be either P or M, who may differ in various ways but can be treated symmetrically with respect to the meeting technology, which allows us to specify that technology rather generally. It may be useful to compare the market structure here with that in Figure 2, where one might say the former concerns temporal separation and the latter spatial separation.

This structure is nice because history independence makes it about as tractable as a typical three-period model, and so without too much additional work we can consider infinite-horizon models. The infinite horizon is critical under standard assumptions if, e.g., one wants to support exchange using fiat currency or support unsecured credit.

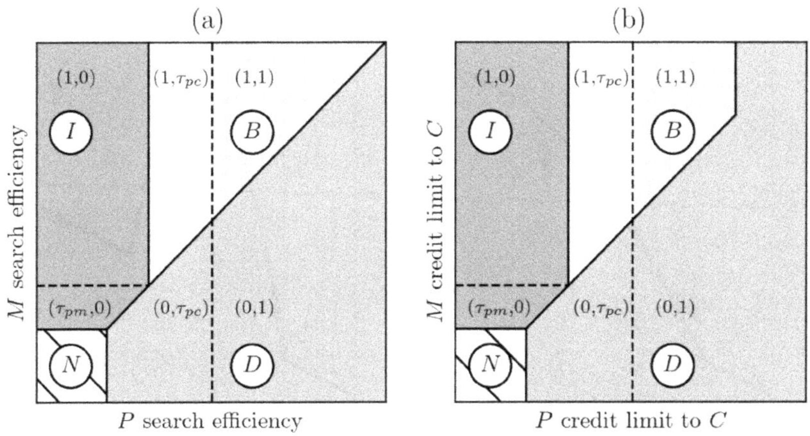

Figure 8 Equilibrium set in search efficiency (panel (a)) and credit limit (panel (b)).

Gong and Wright (2024) show that with exogenous debt limits, equilibrium exists and is unique. Also, they show that one of four trading patterns, called regimes, will emerge: no trade (Regime N); direct trade only (Regime D); indirect trade only (Regime I); or both direct and indirect trade (Regime B). Panel (a) of Figure 8 illustrates how the outcome depends on search efficiency. When search efficiency is low, the market shuts down; when it is moderately higher, the exchange pattern depends on the relative advantage of P and M in search efficiency and bargaining power. If M has no advantage over P, there is no gain from WM trade and we get Regime D. If M has an advantage, WM trade occurs if M meets P, and P that fails to trade in WM may either enter or skip RM depending on search efficiency, corresponding to Regimes B and I.[33]

With divisible goods, bargaining power shapes not only the division of surplus but also its size. Specifically, greater seller bargaining power raises buyer payments but also increases the equilibrium quantity/quality of x. As a result, higher bargaining power for P and M can improve C's payoff – a novel insight in the sense that it cannot happen with indivisible goods. But the bigger contribution may be to introduce a new dimension along which middlemen may have advantages: They are better at using credit, by more reliably promising future payment or enforcing payment by others. This can be captured with exogenous debt limits by saying the limit when M buys x from P – call it

[33] Gong and Wright (2024) discuss monetary exchange in their setup but do not present details. Urias (2018) is better on that, but, as mentioned, he does not let, on our notation, P go to RM, so the only possibility for trade is Regime I. This would appear to be a fruitful area for future research.

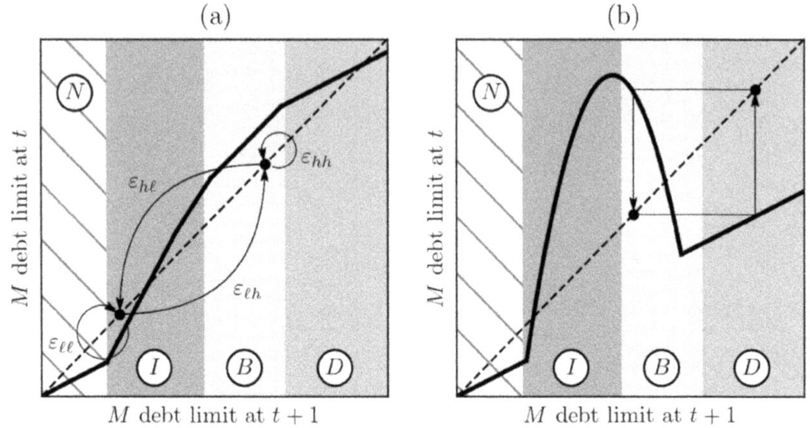

Figure 9 Dynamics: Stochastic (panel (a)) and deterministic (panel (b)) cycles.

D_{pm} – is big or the limit when M sells to C is bigger than when P sells to C – say $D_{mc} > D_{pc}$.[34] One can also consider credit more along the lines of Kiyotaki and Moore (1997), where the mechanism takes away assets, instead of future credit, from renegers.

If the debt limits are sufficiently big, promises of payment in the next CM are perfect substitutes for spot payments in WM and RM in terms of transferable utility. Clearly, it is interesting to make these limits endogenous. Assuming agents cannot commit to any future payments, Gong et al. (2025)[35] support credit without commitment with endogenous debt limits by assuming renegers lose access to future credit, as in many models following Kehoe and Levine (1993). As is known in the literature, this can generate multiple equilibria and endogenous cycles driven by self-fulfilling prophecies. Depending on details, these cycles can be stochastic or deterministic, can involve regime switching, and can be amplified or attenuated by middlemen's activity.

Figure 9 shows two examples, both with three steady-state equilibria. Panel (a) presents a stochastic cycle depending on a two-state sunspot process with probability ε_{ij} transiting from state i to j. Panel (b) presents a deterministic

[34] This is realistic. Consider trying to sell your car. If potential buyers do not have sufficient liquidity for immediate settlement, deferred payment is an option, but you might worry about them reneging. An alternative is to sell your car to a dealer, where default can be less of a concern, either because they have more cash on hand for immediate settlement or becasue they are less likely to renege on deferred settlement. Of course, when dealers sell, their customers may have commitment issues, but it is no stretch to think used-car dealers are better than you at collecting debt.

[35] Gong, X., Qiao, Z., Wong, Y., and Wright, R. (2025) "Intermediation and imperfect credit," unpublished working paper.

cycle driven solely by beliefs but still imposing rational expectations.[36] The example on the left has M amplifying cycles – in the H state, more M enter, and they bring more x – while the example on the right has M attenuating cycles – with M exiting in the H state and entering in the L state. The point is not that intermediation causes instability. Rather, limited commitment gives intermediation an endogenous role, plus it provides an internal source of dynamics, as is known from other work (Gu et al. 2013). This suggests a more nuanced but still interesting link between intermediation and volatility.

Moving from credit back to money, another way to think about the connection with middlemen is to consider Kiyotaki and Wright (1989). It has infinitely lived agents meeting bilaterally at random. There are three goods: $i = 1,2,3$. There are three types, A_1, A_2, and A_3, where A_i consume good i for utility u and produce good $i+1$ modulo 3 (i.e., A_3 produces good 1) at 0 cost, for simplicity. Goods are indivisible and storable one unit at a time. Agents cannot commit and are anonymous, ruling out credit without commitment, so quid pro quo is necessary for exchange.

Good i has a return ρ_i, which could be positive or negative as long as $|\rho_i|$ is not too big. Then A_i always accepts good i in trade and consumes it. The relevant question is: Will A_i trade good $i+1$ for good $i+2$ in an attempt to facilitate acquisition of good i? Or will A_i hold onto good $i+1$ and only trade directly for good i? Let τ_i be the probability A_i trades good $i+1$ for good $i+2$. If $\tau_i > 0$, then type i agents use good $i+2$ as a medium of exchange – they acquire it as a step toward getting their final good i.

A symmetric and stationary strategy profile is $\tau = (\tau_1, \tau_2, \tau_3)$. We also need the distribution of inventories, since A_i can be holding good $i+1$ or $i+2$. It is routine to compute the steady state of this system given any τ. The dynamic programming equations for V_{ij} are also standard, where V_{ij} is i's value function when holding good j. The best response condition for A_1, for example, are: $\tau_1 = 1$ if $V_{13} > V_{12}$; $\tau_1 = 0$ if $V_{13} < V_{12}$; and $\tau_1 = [0,1]$ if $V_{13} = V_{12}$. There are symmetric conditions for the other types. After a little work, one discovers A_1, for example, faces two factors in choosing τ_1: There is a return differential $\rho_3 - \rho_2$ from holding good 3 rather than good 2; and there is a liquidity differential which is the difference in the probability of getting good 1 when holding good 3 rather than good 2, which is endogenous, depending on others' strategies.

[36] When the difference equation crosses the 45° line from below, one can always construct two-state sunspot equilibria but never deterministic cycles. On the other hand, when the difference equation crosses the 45° line from above with slope magnitude greater than 1, deterministic cycles exist in addition to possible sunspot cycles. Again, see Azariadis (1993) for textbook treatment of the relevant dynamical system theory.

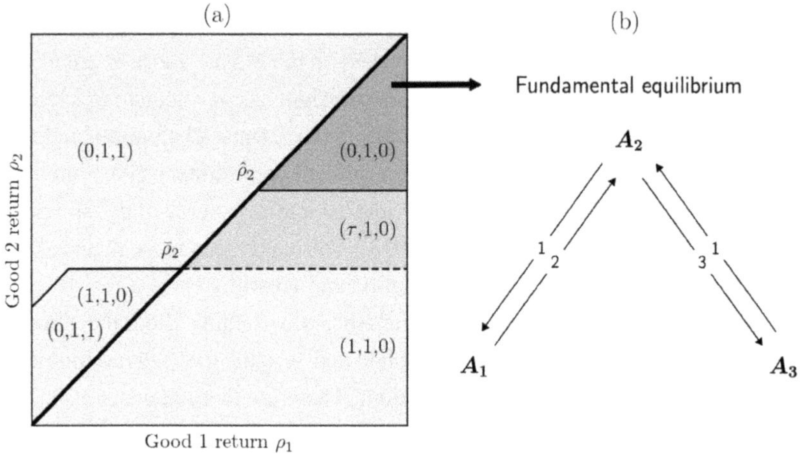

Figure 10 Equilibrium set (panel (a)) and market structure (panel (b)) in Kiyotaki–Wright.

A stationary, symmetric equilibrium is a list of the usual objects satisfying the usual conditions. Assume $\rho_1, \rho_2 > 0 = \rho_3$, so we can display outcomes in the positive quadrant of (ρ_1, ρ_2) space, and assume equal numbers of all types (although it is interesting to consider more general populations as in, e.g., Wright 1995). Figure 10 shows different regions labeled by τ to indicate different regimes that constitute equilibria.

There are two cases, Model A or B, distinguished by $\rho_1 > \rho_2$ or $\rho_2 > \rho_1$ (this exhausts the possibilities since anything else would be a relabeling). In Figure 10, Model A corresponds to the region below the 45° line, where there are two possibilities: If $\rho_2 \geq \hat{\rho}_2$ the unique outcome is $\tau = (0, 1, 0)$; and if $\rho_2 \leq \bar{\rho}_2$ it is $\tau = (1, 1, 0)$. To understand this, note that for A_1 good 3 is more liquid than good 2 since A_3 accepts good 3 but not good 2, and A_3 agents always have what A_1 wants. In contrast, A_2 agents always accept good 2 but only have good 1 with certain probability. Hence, good 3 allows A_1 agents to consume sooner. If $\rho_2 > \hat{\rho}_2$ this liquidity factor does not compensate for a lower return; if $\rho_2 < \hat{\rho}_2$ it does. The reason A_1 is pivotal here is this: For A_2, trading good 3 for good 1 enhances both liquidity and return, as does holding onto good 1 for A_3. Hence, only A_1 has a tradeoff.

In Model A, $\tau = (0, 1, 0)$ is called a fundamental equilibrium that has good 1 as the universally accepted commodity money. It also has A_2 acting as middlemen – they acquire good 1 from its producers and deliver it to its consumers – as shown in panel (b) of Figure 10 (see also Camera 2001, who has endogenous intermediation using the same preference structure, but with divisible goods). This should remind readers of the market structure in Figure 2 from the Rubinstein–Wolinsky model.

However, if $\rho_2 < \bar{\rho}_2$ we instead get $\tau = (1, 1, 0)$, called a speculative equilibrium, which has A_1 trading good 2 for the lower-return good 3 to improve their liquidity position, and both good 1 and 3 are used in indirect exchange. Theory delivers cutoffs for A_1 to sacrifice return for liquidity, but there is a gap: For $\hat{\rho}_2 > \rho_2 > \bar{\rho}_2$ there is no stationary, symmetric equilibrium in pure strategies, but one can show there is one in mixed strategies and nonstationary equilibria with τ cycling over time (Kehoe et al. 1993).

Model B is similar, except that there is always an equilibrium in pure strategies, and for some ρs there are multiple equilibria in pure strategies. There can also be multiplicity for other configurations in mixed strategies for Models A and B. The coexistence of equilibria with different transactions patterns and liquidity properties shows that these are not necessarily pinned down by fundamentals.

Viewing Rubinstein–Wolinsky and Kiyotaki–Wright side by side reveals a connection between middlemen and money. Both arise in the presence of trade frictions, whether from search, information, commitment, etcetera. In these models, *who trades with whom* is central, something that is ignored in the classical, frictionless general equilibrium framework. In the models studied here, middlemen and money share economic concern: facilitating exchange. Despite these parallels, middlemen and money differ in other ways.[37] While the literature has advanced substantially on both topics in isolation, their interaction is an open area for research.

10 Other Contributions

We cannot present the details of all the interesting papers out there, but can provide a broad overview of some. Bose and Sengupta (2010) study a version where middlemen are immediately available to buyers and cater to repeat clientele. Tse (2011) has a setup where agents are dispersed over space and trading costs increase with distance, and shows that middlemen cluster at central locations, thereby increasing trade and welfare. Carapella and Monnet (2020) study how dealers help to reduce counterparty risk, while Gottardi et al. (2019) model counterparty plus asset risk under repo intermediation.

Some papers emphasize the difference between brokers and dealers: The former execute trades on behalf of others while the latter trade on their own behalf. In some models, middlemen set bid and ask prices, including Yavas (1992), Spulber (1996b), van Raalte and Webers (1998), Rust and Hall (2003),

[37] In particular, money is an institution while middlemen are strategic agents, so the equilibrium characterizations for these models can depend on different conditions.

Caillaud and Julien (2003), and Loertscher (2007). Spulber (1996b) characterizes bid-ask spreads in a dynamic model. See also Yavas (1994, 1996), which features brokers that get traders together, like real estate agents and employment agencies.

Another form of intermediation is the market-making platform, like Amazon, eBay, Uber, and Airbnb. These maintain a marketplace and take a commission in return. To understand this, Kultti et al. (2021) consider endogenous platforms that coordinate meetings. Gautier et al. (2023) model an agent's decision to operate as a dealer, a platform, or both based on matching efficiency, inventory risk, and pricing power. Regarding matching efficiency, Teh et al. (2024) study platforms' meeting algorithms in a directed search framework and show that limiting seller exposure to buyers can improve efficiency. Beyond market making, some platforms provide transaction and credit services, which is studied in Han et al. (2024)[38] and Hu et al. (2025).[39] Hagiu and Jullien (2011) model intermediaries that divert consumer search, another role of platforms.

As middlemen play prominent roles in various industries, some papers try explicitly to capture specific institutional contexts rather than describing abstract, general models. Biglaiser et al. (2020), for example, show how information asymmetries and assortative matching help explain empirical findings in used-car markets. Gavazza (2016) examines business aircraft, Leslie and Sorensen (2014) study brokers of tickets to rock concerts, while Antras and Costinot (2011) investigate the impact of middlemen in international trade. Afonso and Lagos (2015) and Bech and Monnet (2016) model endogenous intermediation in interbank money markets. Geromichalos and Jung (2018) study how intermediation affects bid-ask spreads and trade volume in the foreign exchange market.

In early papers, agent heterogeneity is highly stylized. Recent advancements push this boundary in several directions. Hugonnier et al. (2022) allow arbitrary heterogeneity in flow payoffs and derive closed-form formulas for equilibrium outcomes. Uslu (2019) has heterogeneity along three simultaneous dimensions – preferences, inventories, and arrival rates – and shows that the latter is the main driver of intermediation patterns. Bethune et al. (2022) model OTC markets where agents exhibit continuous heterogeneity in valuation and screening ability. Farboodi et al. (2023) begin with ex ante identical agents and characterize continuous heterogeneity in equilibrium search intensity.

---

[38] Han, H., Hu, B., and Watanabe, M. (2024) "From cash to buy-now-pay-later: Impacts of platform-provided credit on market efficiency," unpublished working paper.

[39] Hu, B., Watanabe, M., and Zhang, J. (2025) "A model of supplier finance," unpublished working paper.

Although we focus mainly on models using a search theory, other approaches can also address the role of middlemen. Townsend (1978) argues that multilateral trade is costly and thus intermediation emerges as a core allocation. Also examining core allocations, Kalai et al. (1978) study market efficiency under coalitions connected by middlemen. Manea (2018) analyzes how network structure affects trade along different intermediation paths. Kotowski and Leister (2019) study network formation and show that free entry and competition may fail to eliminate redundant intermediaries. Chang and Zhang (2021)[40] model endogenous network hierarchy with implications for centrality and markups. Chiu et al. (2020) and Farboodi (2023) model the interbank market and show that endogenous intermediation is a key determinant of the core–periphery network and equilibrium efficiency.

In summary, there is a great deal of good work in this area. While we cannot do justice to it all here, we have at least catalogued places where one can look for more.

11 Conclusion

This Element has presented various models and ideas in the economics literature using search and related tools to study middlemen. We focused on theory, neglecting empirical work in the interest of space, but there is certainly some good work on that and room for even more. One takeaway is that many interesting and tractable models have been developed, but there is also more that can be done in terms of theory. We hope this Element encourages further research.

40 Chang, B., and Zhang, S. (2021) “Endogenous Market Making and Network Formation,” unpublished working paper.

References

Afonso, G., and Lagos, R. (2015) "Trade dynamics in the market for federal funds," *Econometrica* 83(1), 263–313.

Aguirregabiria, V. (1999) "The dynamics of markups and inventories in retailing firms," *Review of Economic Studies* 66, 275–308.

Ahn, J., Khandelwal, A. K., and Wei, S. J. (2011) "The role of intermediaries in facilitating trade," *Journal of International Economics* 84, 73–85.

Akerlof, G. A. (1970) "The market for lemons: Quality uncertainty and the market mechanism," *Quarterly Journal of Economics* 84, 488–500.

Albano, G. L., and Lizzeri, A. (2001) "Strategic certification and the provision of quality," *International Economic Review* 42, 267–283.

Allen, F., Morris, S., and Postlewaite, A. (1993) "Finite bubbles with short sale constraints and asymmetric information," *Journal of Economic Theory* 61, 206–229.

Antras, P., and Costinot, A. (2011) "Intermediated trade," *Quarterly Journal of Economics* 126, 1319–1374.

Awaya, Y., Iwasaki, K., and Watanabe, M. (2022) "Rational bubbles and middlemen," *Theoretical Economics* 17, 1559–1587.

Azariadis, C. (1993) *Intertemporal Macroeconomics.* Blackwell.

Baye, M. R., Morgan J., and Scholten, P. (2006) "Information, search, and price dispersion," *Handbook on Economics and Information Systems* vol. 1, Emerald Publishing Limited: 323–375.

Bech, M., and Monnet, C. (2016) "A search-based model of the interbank money market and monetary policy implementation," *Journal of Economic Theory* 164, 32–67.

Bernard, A. B., Jensen, J. B., Redding, S. J., and Schott, P. K. (2007) "Firms in international trade," *Journal of Economic Perspectives* 21, 105–130.

Bethune, Z., Choi, M., and Wright, R. (2020) "Frictional goods markets: Theory and applications," *Review of Economic Studies* 87, 691–720.

Bethune, Z., Sultanum, B., and Trachter, N. (2022) "An information-based theory of financial intermediation," *Review of Economic Studies* 89, 2381–2444.

Biglaiser, G. (1993) "Middlemen as experts," *RAND* 24, 212–223.

Biglaiser, G., and Friedman, J. W. (1994) "Middlemen as guarantors of quality," *International Journal of Industrial Organization* 12, 509–531.

Biglaiser, G., and Friedman, J. W. (1999) "Adverse selection with competitive inspection," *Journal of Economics and Management Strategy* 8, 1–32.

Biglaiser, G., and Li, F. (2018) "Middlemen: The good, the bad, and the ugly," *RAND* 49, 3–22.

Biglaiser, G., Li, F., Murry, C., and Zhao, Y. (2020) "Intermediaries and product quality in used car markets," *RAND* 51, 905–933.

Binmore, K. (1992) *Fun and Games: A Text on Game Theory*. D. C. Health.

Bose, G., and Sengupta, A. (2010) "A dynamic model of search and intermediation," *UNSW Australian School of Business Research Paper*, https://papers.ssrn.com/sol3/papers.cfm?abstract_id=1550088.

Burdett, K., and Coles, M. G. (1997) "Marriage and class," *Quarterly Journal of Economics* 112, 141–168.

Burdett, K., and Judd, K. L. (1983) "Equilibrium price dispersion," *Econometrica* Jul. 1, 955–969.

Burdett, K., Shi, S., and Wright, R. (2001) "Pricing and matching with frictions," *Journal of Political Economy* 109, 1060–1085.

Caillaud, B., and Julien, B. (2003) "Competing in network industries: Divide and conquer," *RAND* 34, 309–328.

Camera, G. (2001) "Search, dealers, and the terms of trade," *Review of Economic Dynamics* 4(3), 680–694.

Carapella, F., and Monnet, C. (2020) "Dealers' insurance, market structure, and liquidity," *Journal of Financial Economics* 138(3), 725–753.

Cavalcanti, R. D. O., and Wallace, N. (1999) "Inside and outside money as alternative media of exchange," *Journal of Money, Credit and Banking* 31, 443–457.

Chiu, J., Eisenschmidt, J., and Monnet, C. (2020) "Relationships in the interbank market," *Review of Economic Dynamics* 35, 170–191.

Çinlar, E. (1975) *Introduction to Stochastic Processes*. Prentice Hall.

Dana Jr., J. D., and Spier, K. E. (2001) "Revenue sharing and vertical control in the video rental industry," *Journal of Industrial Economics* 49, 223–245.

Davis, S.J. and de la Parra, B.S. (2025) "Application flows," No. w32320. National Bureau of Economic Research.

Diamond, P. A. (1982) "Aggregate demand management in search equilibrium," *Journal of Political Economy* 90, 881–894.

Diamond, D. W., and Dybvig, P. H. (1983) "Bank runs, deposit insurance, and liquidity," *Journal of Political Economy*, 91, 401–419.

Duffie, D., Garleanu, N., and Pederson, L. H. (2005) "Over-the-counter markets," *Econometrica* 73, 1815–1847.

Duffie, D., Garleanu, N., and Pederson, L. H. (2007) "Valuation in over-the-counter markets," *Review of Financial Studies* 20, 1865–9000.

Ellison, G., and Ellison, S. F. (2005) "Lessons about markets from the internet," *Journal of Economic Perspectives* 19, 139–158.

Farboodi, M. (2023) "Intermediation and voluntary exposure to counterparty risk," *Journal of Political Economy* 131(12), 3267–3309.

Farboodi, M., Jarosch, G., Menzio, G., and Wiriadinata, U. (2025) "Intermediation as rent extraction," *Journal of Economic Theory* 106029.

Farboodi, M., Jarosch, G., and Shimer, R. (2023) "The emergence of market structure," *Review of Economic Studies* 90, 261–292.

Garella, P. (1989) "Adverse selection and the middleman," *Economica* 56, 395–399.

Gautier, P., Hu, B., and Watanabe, M. (2023)"Marketmaking middlemen," *RAND* 54, 1–21.

Gavazza, A. (2011) "The role of trading frictions in real asset markets," *American Economic Review* 101, 1106–1143.

Gavazza, A. (2016) "An empirical equilibrium model of a decentralized asset market," *Econometrica* 84, 1755–1798.

Gehrig, T. (1993) "Intermediation in search markets," *Journal of Economics and Management Strategy* 2, 97–120.

Geromichalos, A. (2012) "Directed search and optimal production," Journal of Economic Theory, 147(6), 2303–2331.

Geromichalos, A. (2014) "Directed search and the Bertrand paradox," International Economic Review, 55(4), 1043–1065.

Geromichalos, A., and Jung, K. (2018) "An over-the-counter approach to the forex market," *International Economic Review* 59, 859–905.

Glode, V., and Opp, C. (2016) "Asymmetric information and intermediation chains," *American Economic Review* 106, 2699–2721.

Gong, X. (2018) "Middlemen in search models with intensive and extensive margins," https://asset.library.wisc.edu/1711.dl/AXYDG5BVJPCPR8Q/R/file-7495b.pdf.

Gong, X., and Wright, R. (2024) "Middlemen in search equilibrium with intensive and extensive margins," *International Economic Review* 65, 1657–1679.

Gong, X., Qiao, Z., and Wright, R. (2024) "Middlemen redux," *Journal of Economic Behavior & Organization* 240, 107345.

Gottardi, P., Maurin, V., and Monnet, C. (2019) "A theory of repurchase agreements, collateral re-use, and repo intermediation," *Review of Economic Dynamics* 33, 30–56.

Gu, C., Mattesini, F., Monnet, C., and Wright, R. (2013) "Endogenous credit cycles," *Journal of Political Economy* 121, 803–1005.

Gu, C., Monnet, C., Nosal, E., and Wright, R. (2023) "Diamond-Dybvig and beyond: On the instability of banking," *European Economic Review* 154, 104414.

Gu, C., Wang L., and Wright, R. (2026) "Intermediaries, inventories and endogenous dynamics," *Journal of Economic Theory* 231, 106113.

Hagiu, A., and Jullien, B. (2011) "Why do intermediaries divert search?" *RAND* 42, 337–362.

Hugonnier, J., Lester, B., and Weill, P. O. (2020) "Frictional intermediation in over-the-counter markets," *Review of Economic Studies* 87, 1432–1469.

Hugonnier, J., Lester, B., and Weill, P. O. (2022) "Heterogeneity in decentralized asset markets," *Theoretical Economics* 17, 1313–1356.

Hugonnier, J., Lester, B., and Weill, P. O. (2025) *The Economics of Over-the-Counter Markets: A Toolkit for the Analysis of Decentralized Exchange*. Princeton University Press.

Johri, A., and Leach, J. (2002) "Middlemen and the allocation of heterogeneous goods," *International Economic Review* 43, 347–361.

Jovanovic, B., and Menkveld, A. J. (2024) "Middlemen in limit order markets," *SSRN Working Paper* 1624329.

Kalai, E., Postlewaite, A., and Roberts, J. (1978) "Barriers to trade and disadvantageous middlemen: Nonmonotonicity of the core," *Journal of Economic Theory* 19, 200–209.

Kariv, S., Kotowski, M. H., and Leister, C. M. (2018) "Liquidity risk in sequential trading networks," *Games and Economic Behavior* 109, 565–581.

Kehoe, T. J., Kiyotaki, N., and Wright, R. (1993) "More on money as a medium of exchange," *Economic Theory* 3, 297–314.

Kehoe, T. J., and Levine, D. K. (1993) "Debt-constrained asset markets," *Review of Economic Studies* 60, 865–888.

Kiyotaki, N., and Moore, J. (1997) "Credit cycles," *Journal of Political Economy* 105, 211–248.

Kiyotaki, N., and Wright, R. (1989) "On money as a medium of exchange," *Journal of Political Economy* 97, 927–954.

Kotowski, M. H., and Leister, C. M. (2019) "Trading networks and equilibrium intermediation," *HKS Working Paper* RWP18-001.

Kultti, K., Takalo, T., and Vahamaa, O. (2021) "Intermediation in a directed search model," *Journal of Economics and Management Strategy* 30, 456–471.

Lagos, R., and Rocheteau, G. (2006) "Search in asset markets," *American Economic Review* 97, 198–202.

Lagos, R., and Rocheteau, G. (2009) "Liquidity in asset markets with search frictions," *Econometrica* 77(2), 403–426.

Lagos, R., Rocheteau, G., and Wright, R. (2017) "Liquidity: A new monetarist perspective," *Journal of Economic Literature* 55, 371–440.

Lagos, R., and Wright, R. (2005) "A unified framework for monetary theory and policy analysis," *Journal of Political Economy* 113, 463–484.

Leslie, P. (2004) "Price discrimination in Broadway theaters," *RAND* 35, 520–541.

Leslie, P., and Sorensen, A. (2014) "Resale and rent-seeking: An application to ticket markets," *Review of Economic Studies* 81, 266–300.

Lester, B., Shourideh, A., Venkateswaran, V., and Zetlin-Jones, A. (2023) "Market-making with search and information frictions," *Journal of Economic Theory* 212, 105714.

Lester, B., Visschers, L., and Wolthoff, R. (2017) "Competing with asking prices," *Theoretical Economics* 12, 731–770.

Li, D., and Schurhoff, N. (2019) "Dealer networks," *Journal of Finance* 74, 91–144.

Li, F., Murry, C., Tian, C., and Zhou, Y. (2024) "Inventory management in decentralized markets," *International Economic Review* 65, 431–470.

Li, Y. (1998) "Middlemen and private information," *Journal of Monetary Economics* 42, 131–159.

Li, Y. (1999) "Money and middlemen in an economy with private information," *Economic Inquiry* 37, 1–12.

Lizzeri, A. (1999) "Information revelation and certification intermediaries," *RAND* 30, 214–231.

Loertscher, S. (2007) "Horizontally differentiated market makers," *Journal of Economics and Management Strategy* 16, 793–825.

Lucas, R. E. (1980) "Equilibrium in a pure currency economy," *Economic Inquiry* 18, 203–220.

Lucas, R. E., and Prescott, E. C. (1974) "Equilibrium search and unemployment," *Journal of Economic Theory* 7, 188–209.

Manea, M. (2018) "Intermediation and resale in networks," *Journal of Political Economy* 126, 1250–1301.

Masters, A. (2007) "Middlemen in search equilibrium," *International Economic Review* 48, 343–362.

Masters, A. (2008) "Unpleasant middlemen," *Journal of Economic Behavior and Organization* 68, 73–86.

Monieson, D. D. (2010) "A historical survey concerning marketing middlemen as producers of value," *Journal of Historical Research in Marketing* 2, 218–226.

Moraga-Gonzalez, J. L., and Watanabe, M. (2023) "Price equilibrium with selling constraints," *CESifo Working Paper* 10583.

Mortensen, D. T., and Pissarides, C. A. (1999) "New developments in models of search in the labor market," *Handbook of Labor Economics* 3, 2567–2627.

Nosal, E., Wong, Y., and Wright, R. (2015) "More on middlemen: Equilibrium entry and efficiency in markets with intermediation," *Journal of Money, Credit and Banking* 47, 7–37.

Nosal, E., Wong, Y., and Wright, R. (2019) "Intermediation in markets for goods and markets for assets," *Journal of Economic Theory* 183, 876–906.

Pissarides, C. A. (2000) *Equilibrium Unemployment Theory*. MIT Press.

Philippon, T. (2015) "Has the US finance industry become less efficient? On the theory and measurement of financial intermediation," *American Economic Review* 105, 1408–1438.

Rand, A. (1971) The Fountainhead. The New American Library, Inc.

Rhodes, A., Watanabe, M., and Zhou, J. (2021) "Multiproduct intermediaries," *Journal of Political Economy* 129, 421–464.

Rocheteau, G., and Nosal, E. (2017) *Money, Payments, and Liquidity*. MIT Press.

Rocheteau, G., and Wright, R. (2005) "Money in search equilibrium, in competitive equilibrium, and in competitive search equilibrium," *Econometrica* 73, 175–202.

Rocheteau, G., and Wright, R. (2013) "Liquidity and asset-market dynamics," *Journal of Monetary Economics* 60, 275–294.

Rossman, M. L. (1984) "Export trading company legislation: US response to Japanese foreign market penetration," *Journal of Small Business Management* 22, 62–66.

Rubinstein, A., and Wolinsky, A. (1987) "Middlemen," *Quarterly Journal of Economics* 102, 581–594.

Rust, J., and Hall, G. (2003) "Middlemen versus market makers: A theory of competitive exchange," *Journal of Political Economy* 111, 353–403.

Shevchenko, A. (2004) "Middlemen," *International Economic Review* 45, 1–24.

Shi, S. (1995) "Money and prices: A model of search and bargaining," *Journal of Economic Theory* 67, 467–496.

Shi, S. (1997) "A divisible search model of fiat money," *Econometrica* 65, 75–102.

Smith, E. (2004) "Intermediated search," *Economica* 71, 619–636.

Spulber, D. F. (1996a) "Market microstructure and intermediation," *Journal of Economic Perspectives* 10, 135–152.

Spulber, D. F. (1996b) "Market making by price-setting firms," *Review of Economic Studies*, 63, 559–580.

Spulber, D. F. (1999) *Market Microstructure: Intermediaries and the Theory of the Firm*. Cambridge University Press.

Spulber, D. F. (2002) "Market microstructure and incentives to invest," *Journal of Political Economy* 110, 352–381.

Teh, C., Wang, C., and Watanabe, M. (2024) "Strategic limitation of market accessibility: Search platform design and welfare," *Journal of Economic Theory* 216, 105798.

Townsend, R. M. (1978) "Intermediation with costly bilateral exchange," *Review of Economic Studies* 45, 417–425.

Trejos, A., and Wright, R. (1995) "Search, bargaining, money, and prices," *Journal of Political Economy* 103, 118–141.

Trejos, A., and Wright, R. (2016) "Search-based models of money and finance: An integrated approach," *Journal of Economic Theory* 164, 10–31.

Tse, C. Y. (2011) "The spatial origin of commerce," *International Economic Review* 52, 349–377.

Turner, S. (1836) *The History of the Anglo-Saxons: From the Earliest Period to the Norman Conquest*, Longman, Rees, Orme, Brown, Green & Longman.

Urias, M. (2018) "Search frictions, limited commitment and middlemen," https://escholarship.org/uc/item/76g664pg.

Üslü, S. (2019) "Pricing and liquidity in decentralized asset markets," *Econometrica* 87, 2079–2140.

Van Raalte, C., and Webers, H. (1998) "Spatial competition with intermediated matching," *Journal of Economic Behavior and Organization* 3, 477–488.

Watanabe, M. (2010) "A model of merchants," *Journal of Economic Theory* 145, 1865–1689.

Watanabe, M. (2018) "Middlemen: The visible market makers," *Japanese Economic Review* 69, 156–170.

Watanabe, M. (2020) "Middlemen: A directed search equilibrium approach," *BE Journal of Macroeconomics* 20, 20190258.

Weill, P. O. (2007) "Leaning against the wind," *Review of Economic Studies* 74, 1329–1354.

Weill, P. O. (2008) "Liquidity premia in dynamic bargaining markets," *Journal of Economic Theory* 140, 66–96.

Williamson, S., and Wright, R. (1994) "Barter and monetary exchange under private information," *American Economic Review* 84, 104–123.

Wong, T. N. (2016) "A tractable monetary model under general preferences," *Review of Economic Studies* 83, 402–420.

Wright, R. (1995) "Search, evolution, and money," *Journal of Economic Dynamics and Control* 19, 181–206.

Wright, R., Kircher, P., Julien, B., and Guerrieri, V. (2021) "Directed search and competitive search equilibrium: A guided tour," *Journal of Economic Literature* 59, 90–148.

Wright, R., and Wong, Y. (2014) "Buyers, sellers and middlemen: Variations on search-theoretic themes," *International Economic Review* 55, 375–397.

Yavas, A. (1992) "Marketmakers versus matchmakers," *Journal of Financial Intermediation* 2, 33–58.

Yavas, A. (1994) "Middlemen in bilateral search markets," *Journal of Labor Economics* 12, 406–429.

Yavas, A. (1996) "Search and trading in intermediated markets," *Journal of Economics and Management Strategy* 5, 195–216.

Acknowledgement

We thank Chao Gu, Kohei Iwasaki, Yiting Li, Gary Biglaiser, Bo Hu, Makoto Watanabe, and Maryam Farboodi for input. We also thank two anonymous referees for very helpful comments. Gong acknowledges the support from the Natural Science Foundation of China (No.72503222), and the Humanities and Social Sciences Project of the Ministry of Education of China (No.24YJC790052). Wright acknowledges support from the Ray Zemon Chair in Liquid Assets and the Ken Burdett Professorship in Search Theory and Applications at University of Wisconsin-Madison. The usual disclaimers apply.

Cambridge Elements

Money and Banking

Chao Gu
University of Missouri

Chao Gu has been Professor at the University of Missouri since she graduated from Cornell University with a PhD in Economics in 2007. Her research interests are macroeconomics and monetary economics. She has published in top journals such as Econometrica, Journal of Political Economy, Review of Economic Studies, Journal of Monetary Economics, Journal of Economic Theory, and more.

Joseph Haslag
Auburn University

Joseph Haslag is the Donald Street Professor and Department Head in the Department of Economics at Auburn University. Before his appointment at Auburn, Dr. Haslag served in the Economics Departments at University of Missouri-Columbia, Michigan State University, Southern Methodist University and as a researcher at the Federal Reserve Bank of Dallas. He has written extensively on macroeconomic and monetary topics.

About the Series

This Element series is an outlet for current research on money, banking, payment systems and monetary policy. Elements in the series will consist of a combination of literature reviews and frontier research.

Cambridge Elements

Money and Banking

Elements in the Series

Monetary Policy Implementation
Stephen Williamson

Middlemen in Search Equilibrium: A Survey
Grace Xun Gong, Ziqi Qiao, and Randall Wright

A full series listing is available at: www.cambridge.org/EMAB

For EU product safety concerns, contact us at Calle de José Abascal, 56–1°, 28003 Madrid, Spain or eugpsr@cambridge.org.

www.ingramcontent.com/pod-product-compliance
Ingram Content Group UK Ltd.
Pitfield, Milton Keynes, MK11 3LW, UK
UKHW021921220726
473566UK00010B/403
* 9 7 8 1 0 0 9 7 0 0 2 7 6 *